DUALITY
INTO
UNITY

DUALITY
INTO
UNITY

A Spiritual & Social Vision
For the Millennium

NICK BAMFORTH

AMETHYST BOOKS

NEW YORK   LONDON

AMETHYST BOOKS

P.O. Box 895,
Woodstock, N.Y.12498,
U.S.A.

Lime Tree House,
Swalcliffe, Banbury,
Oxfordshire, OX15 5EH
England

Library of Congress Catalog Card Number: 92-71241

Hardcover ISBN 0-944256-03-1
Paperback ISBN 0-944256-24-4

Amethyst Books are distributed in the
United States by the Talman Company, New York,
and in the United Kingdom and Europe by
Ashgrove Distribution, Bath.

Design by Paperweight

Typeset by Falcon Graphic Art Ltd

Printed in the United States of America.

Acknowledgments

I would like to thank the many people who have had a profound influence on my life and whose interaction with me has shaped my view of the world. They know who they are.

In addition, I would like to acknowledge three writers who have had a major bearing on the genesis of this book:

Julian Jaynes, whose book *The Origin of Consciousness in the Breakdown of the Bicameral Mind* planted the seeds for this book many years ago, even though we may come to somewhat different conclusions.

Joseph Campbell, whose three books, *Primitive Mythology, Oriental Mythology* and *Occidental Mythology*, furnished the research for much of what I write about in the first three chapters and whose style and imagination were an inspiration in themselves.

Eric Morse, whose ideas in *The Living Stars* and *What On Earth Is Happening?* gave me an excellent focus for what was whirling around in my head at the time.

Contents

Acknowledgements   5

Introduction   9

Part One: Unity into Duality

    Chapter 1: Creation and the Dawning of
        Consciousness   15

    Chapter 2: The Rise of the Sequential
        Mind   23

    Chapter 3: Man and God   47

    Chapter 4: Egypt and the Decline of a
        Civilization   55

    Chapter 5: Greece and the Secularization
        of Thought   69

    Chapter 6: Christianity: The Religion of
        Power   97

    Chapter 7: The Middle Ages and the

Stirring of the Individual   107

Chapter 8: Renaissance, Reformation and
   Rationalism   119

Chapter 9: Materialism and Fear   125

Part Two: Duality into Unity

Chapter 1: A Matter of Life and Death   137

Chapter 2: Man, Earth and the
   Universe   145

Chapter 3: The Unity of Love and the
   Power of the Dark Side   155

Chapter 4: Sex and Sexuality   171

Chapter 5: Relationships, Parents and
   Children   183

Chapter 6: Education   195

Chapter 7: Government   205

Chapter 8: Reconciliation and
   Transformation   221

Bibliography   229

Index   231

Introduction

The apparent opposites of duality pervade every aspect of our existence – from the primeval concepts of order and chaos or good and evil to the fundamental divisions which we have created between the rational and the intuitive or the physical and the spiritual – and yet, very few people seem to be aware of how such distinctions have come to be so deeply etched within the human psyche.

It continuously strikes me what a fearful creature Western Man is, despite all his material progress, his technology, his belief in his ability to control his environment. We find it so much easier to see things in terms of black and white, rather than focus on the infinite shades of grey in between or see an interdependence in all things. Every moment of our lives, we observe the diversity of existence around us, the continuous mobility of change and renewal in nature; and yet most of us choose to hide behind the rigid barriers of conformity and immutability which we allow our society to build around us, rather than explore the endless possibilities which stretch out before us.

I believe that this mentality which dominates our world has brought us very close to a crisis point where the whole future of humanity hangs in the balance, and the purpose of this book is to show how it is that we have reached such a point and what we can do about it.

Part One illustrates how we as a species have fundamentally strayed away from an innate sense of Unity with our fellow beings and with the greater Source of our being. I do not judge this process, as this division from Unity into Duality is the very essence of our evolution and is inextricably linked with the expansion of our consciousness as we explore the boundaries of human experience. To judge our past behavior would be to negate the lessons we have learned along the way.

However, we have now reached a point where the divisions of our world have become so pronounced that we risk upsetting the natural balance which exists upon this Earth, so it is now time for us to bring a sense of Unity back into our existence. The ways in which we can do this and bring a deeper state of harmony back into our world are the focus of Part Two.

My approach is necessarily Western, as it is the Western, or, more to the point, the white man's ethic which dominates the world at this particular time and which has brought us to this present state of crisis. As I chart the course of the development of Unity into Duality, you will note that my history of human civilization is very personal and subjective, in that I focus on what I consider to be the 'flashpoints' in the evolution of our human consciousness: those specific locations and periods of extraordinary change and crisis within the human psyche which propel mankind along a completely new and hitherto unexplored path.

I believe that we are now on the brink of such a 'flashpoint', when our great gift of free will is going to be tested to its limits. The essential message of this book is therefore one of responsibility, as it is a matter of collective choice as to whether we decide to continue along our present path of separation from the Unity of Life or recreate a society which is based on a feeling of concern and compassion for one's fellow beings and on an innate understanding on the interdependence of all forms of life. I call this a 'spiritual and social vision', because it is now time to integrate a sense of the spiritual eternity and connectedness of existence into the core of our day-to-day lives and to realize that our every act has an effect not only upon those around us, but also upon a Greater World at large.

True change can only take place when we have the courage

to step beyond the narrow limits of what we have been brought up to believe in and act according to our own conscience. If we fail to do this, we do not have the right to hold governments or anybody but ourselves responsible for what the future will bring. The choice is ours.

Part One

Unity into Duality

Chapter 1

Creation and the Dawning
of Consciousness

When we look back to the origins of mankind, we are immediately confronted by the apparent dualism of Creation and Evolution, thus affording us an initial opportunity to look within ourselves and see how much we are prone to dualistic thinking and the tendency to adhere to one concept to the exclusion of all else.

There are certain people who believe in a literal interpretation of the Creation Story as written down in Genesis in the Old Testament; there are others, forming the majority, who follow the established scientific belief in man's gradual evolution from ape-like creatures. If you fall into either category, those shades of grey mentioned in the Introduction have passed you by!

In today's world, there are few who will question some general theory of Evolution, but there are many who will reject outright the concept of Creation, not understanding that the mysteries which are hidden deep within the Creation myths from around the world offer the key to that special seed which propelled mankind along its singular evolutionary path in the first place. Such an inability to grasp the symbolic nature of myth and the layers of knowledge it conceals is hardly surprising. The Judeo/Christian mind has produced such a fundamental split between the seemingly contradictory realms of 'faith' and 'empirical knowledge' that the true significance of myth as the fusion between the two has been lost to all but a few.

Indeed, if we look at the countless Creation myths which abound throughout the world, the one which is still sometimes perceived as actual historical fact is the story of Genesis. This in itself illustrates how 'religion' has evolved in the West into a monolithic structure full of laws and strictures, rather than the personal, spiritual experience which is instilled in the so-called 'heathen' religions. Instead of experiencing the many glorious levels of the story of the Garden of Eden, Western man has been fed an unpalatable interpretation by institutions whose concerns have more to do with power and control than the inner life of man.

Of course, the Creation of man — in some traditions seen as simultaneous with his Fall — is no simple literal story. It is all about the Dawning of Consciousness within man, what it was that set us apart from other living creatures on this planet. It concerns that certain moment in time, which Jung describes as our 'Psychic Birth', when some momentous event happened which swept our species along the path to this very moment which we are now experiencing in our own lives. Just as the birth of a child is not without pain and trauma, so it was that this 'Psychic Birth' left an indelible imprint on the inner being of mankind.

Many of the ancient myths look back to a Golden Age where man walked and talked with God and with other animals, where all was in harmony and interconnected. This is followed by the 'Fall of Man', sometimes brought about by an abuse of power, as in the story of Atlantis*, sometimes by a seemingly hazardous, catastrophic event — a point at which man as we know him begins to evolve, often looking back in fear at the enormity of what happened, and, in certain cases, burdened by the 'guilt' of his errors which caused his Fall.

The Judeo/Christian myth of the Garden of Eden is weighed

---

*There are countless books on the Fall of Atlantis, and their common theme is of an advanced people blessed with an innate understanding of the cycles of Nature and the Universe, but whose abuse of these gifts for their own individual power ultimately upsets the natural balance they inherited and leads to the destruction of the great civilization they had built.

down by this deep sense of fear and guilt and thus differs from nearly all other Creation myths, in particular those of the East, which do not apportion blame for the 'Fall of Man'. In this Western Creation story of the Old Testament, there are three elements which stand in direct opposition to the more fluid Creation myths which abound in other, more mystical traditions.

First of all, it is an external God who creates Man; then, it is this same external Being who creates Woman out of a part of Man; and, finally, it is Woman who is responsible for the Fall – a reflection of the extent to which the female creative power had been debased and suppressed in the Judaic culture by the time this myth came to be written down.

On the other hand, in most Eastern and mystical traditions, God is not perceived as being separate from man. In the first chapter of his *Oriental Mythology*, Joseph Campbell documents how, in one of the Indian Creation myths, 'the Universe was nothing but the Self in the form of a man.' It is only when He articulates the word 'I' and formulates a consciousness of self that He first feels fear and then a sense of being alone. So, in order to fill this loneliness, it is He who splits Himself in two and makes woman out of Himself. Then, in uniting with His other half, He creates mankind.

In the Garden of Eden, man is created, then woman and there is harmony followed by the Fall. After the Fall, Adam and Eve are driven out of the Garden by the curses of this relentless God, and flee not only in fear, but, even more of consequence, weighed down by the burden of *guilt* for having done 'wrong', for having 'sinned'. The extent of this fear, combined with the weight of guilt, is, as we shall see during the progress of Part One of this book, one of the hallmarks of Western Man.

In the Eastern tradition, it is the very act of creation, of creating two out of one which could be interpreted as the Fall, as this represents a division of the energy of One, so that the figure of One, of God, multiplies and fragments into many pieces. And yet, it is not a Fall at all, as it is all part of the plan, the will to expand and to experience brought to fruition by the Self, rather than by an outside force.

So, within all Eastern religions, there is a Cosmic sense of order (dharma) behind all life, cycles of change which are at the heart of the Universe as well as our individual lives. What continues to feed the duality which was unleashed upon the world is our ego which creates within us an illusory sense of separateness from the Source of All Being. It is our ego which is at the heart of our emotions as we crash around in this world of illusion, experiencing and expanding through our contact with other beings; and, through meditation, yoga or whatever means one uses to find that state of sublime, inner peace, it is the dissolution of the ego which leads the Master back to the Source, to Unity.

Whereas the Eastern mind expands through the experience of duality, sees it as illusion and then turns towards the stillness of Unity, the Western mind is driven along a continuous path of expansion. What lies more strongly than anything behind this urge to succeed and achieve and to experience through every sensation is Western Man's separateness from his Source of being, his God. In seeing God as a Supreme Being who rules from above, he is unable to envision merging with the Source of his Being or even to see his creative energy coming from anything but his own separate individuality, his ego. He takes the mantle of responsibility into his own hands and, in doing so, is driven forward both by courage and by arrogance.

Most Westerners would judge the philosophy of the East as a passive acceptance, an inability to stride forwards and create one's own destiny. In the West, we are always driven forwards; to struggle is our destiny, for, deep within us, we carry that primeval fear and guilt which gives us no rest: the fear of failing once more and the innate need for approval by an external source.

We cannot judge one as being superior to the other. They just are. This is the true essence of duality. Each has its place. Only when they become one and the same, integrated – only then does the cycle come to an end.

If all of us on this planet were of an Eastern mentality, then the experience of the senses, and thereby the growth and expansion of human understanding, would have been minimal, so there would be little duality in the first place. If the Western mentality were to dominate this Earth, as it is doing at this moment, the obsession with individual power would have no bounds, and another catastrophe of immense destruction could bring this particular cycle of life on Earth to an end.

But, more about that later!

Perhaps the most vital symbol in the Garden of Eden is the Serpent, which for so long has been simplistically and literally viewed as Satan, the personification of Evil, the angel cast out from Heaven!

Yet, in all other traditions, the serpent has a diametrically opposed significance. Far from being viewed as a source of evil, it is a symbol of eternal renewal, with its continuous casting off of its own skin, and, in certain cultures, its ability to swallow itself. Even in the Levant, thousands of years before the Book of Genesis was written, the serpent was revered as a deity in its own right; Buddha was protected by a great Serpent King while he sat under the Bodhi Tree – a representation of the universal image of the Cosmic Tree, which, with the serpent wrapped around it, unites the physical world below to the spiritual dimension above; the caduceus of Hermes, the Greek god of mystic knowledge and rebirth, consists of two copulating snakes entwined along a staff. The list is endless and is perfectly documented by Joseph Campbell in his *Masks of God*, in particular in the Serpent's Bride, the first chapter of *Occidental Mythology*.

In all of these traditions, the serpent represents duality as a creative force within the evolution of mankind, most powerfully embodied as knowledge, consciousness and sexuality. In tempting Eve to eat the apple, the serpent did nothing but awaken human consciousness into an awareness of self and set it along the path of discovery and the search for knowledge. In its most primeval guise, it releases the dualistic energy of sexuality, whose immeasurably creative, and sometimes destructive, power lies at the heart of those Creation myths arising from cultures which revel in their sexual energy rather than fear it.

Even in our so-called liberated modern Western society, sex still often inspires fear, guilt and a whole host of confused emotions, the source of which goes back to the supremacy of the Western Christian Church, as we shall see in the relevant chapter. In Western religious tradition, sex has always been viewed as opposed to spirit, as a means simply of procreation. In the East, sex is essential to spirit, with the 'kundalini' energy rising in the adept like a snake spiralling upwards from the base of spine. It is the symbol of the fusion of the physical and spiritual on this earthly plane.

The serpent, continuously changing its skin at regular intervals, is also a symbol of the moon, itself the symbol of rebirth and eternal life, and, just as important in this context, of fertility and the menstrual cycles of a woman. We have become so accustomed to living in a male dominated society that we have forgotten the extent to which the power of female creativity was once respected, with the Mother Earth Goddess being the primary object of worship in all early civilizations, ruling in *harmony* with her male consort, until masculine supremacy swept across the Earth with its exclusive culmination in the Hebrew god Yahweh, the God of the Old Testament.

Those of us living in the West today are inheritors of the mentality which has suppressed the fluid universality of myth and ceremony, replacing it with a rigid dogma and ritual which denies the individual the right to find his or her spiritual connection from within.

There have, of course, been those few voices down the centuries, from the greatest prophets to the simplest folk, who have radiated with their own inner spiritual power and have sought, in their teachings or their own day-to-day existence, to integrate the spiritual into the physical and to base their lives upon the principle of Love: a sense of Unity not only with their fellow men, but also with the Source of all Being. Yet, these voices have ultimately been drowned or suppressed by those forces which have felt threatened by the power which the individual spiritual quest represents.

It would, however, be redundant to blame these forces of control for the state of our world today, for they are no more than a reflection of humanity as a whole. If we blame the government, or organized religion, or anything from which we disassociate ourselves, we are missing the point. The world which you and I inhabit is the result of a remarkable and complex evolution, and we are all part of this evolution – much of which still remains hidden deep within our subconscious. To judge this evolution is to judge and therefore cut ourselves off from the essence of our physical being. This will solve nothing.

On the other hand, if we go back to the very earliest stages of our evolution and follow our progress to this present day, we may learn some lessons as to how we have managed to create the environment we live in today. Some of our history may not appear to be very pretty, as has been the case with much of our more recent behavior, but this does not mean that we must just reject it as a temporary aberration.

We cannot deny our evolution, but, in understanding the forces which have shaped us into what we now are, we can perhaps correct the imbalances which have brought not only our species but the whole planet to a state of crisis.

Such is the aim of this book.

Chapter 2

The Rise of the Sequential Mind

If we look at the myths pertaining to the 'Fall of Man', there is an abundance of association with a 'natural' catastrophe on Earth which sweeps away the old. These include the floods which swept away Atlantis or which destroyed all mankind but Noah and his family, each implying a punishment for man going beyond pre-established limits and using his power to upset the natural balance of life. A modern account of a related but different kind of catastrophe is written by Dr. Eric Morse, theologian, psychologist, astronomer, astrologer, in his books *The Living Stars* and *What On Earth Is Happening?*:*

The story of a stellar explosion very close to Earth and its neighboring planets is told in the works of many early writers: the Romans Ovid and Manilius, the Greeks Plato and Nonnos, the Hindu Vedas, and even earlier well-preserved accounts in south-west Africa and Polynesia. By the Romans and Greeks, the ill-fated star was called Phaethon, or Phaeton, the name revived for

---

*Whether you choose to take this account as a literal truth or as another aspect of myth is up to use. I use it here in order to focus on that particular element within mankind which created the separation between man and other animals: the sequential mind.

it in the 1950s–60s by the Soviet researchers tracing its after-effects on Earth.

Extracting the main features from the varied poetry and mythology, we find that there were once two suns in our local sky, of which only one now remains and is appropriately named Solus or Sol – 'alone' in the 'Solar' system.

Such a pair of stars close together is called a Binary Pair, not to be confused with a 'Double' when two stars far apart simply look to be close as seen from Earth. True binaries are not uncommon in space and are well-known as sources of Nova explosions. What happens then is that one of the pair, usually the smaller, has sucked material from the partner until the gravitational field of the latter can no longer contain the internal pressures of its nuclear furnace. The result is a gigantic atomic explosion destroying the star partially or totally. All that we see from Earth, even with big telescopes, is a very bright light for a few weeks or months, as though a star has just been created – hence the name Nova (New) given to it. But, on a planet near to the stricken star, the destruction is horrific . . .

At all events, when Phaeton reached the zodiacal degree later said to be nineteen of Scorpio by Roman and Greek retelling of earlier records, the impoverished star exploded . . . The degree is still called '*Serpentis*', 'of the snake', by astrologers and counted about the most malefic point in the zodiac. Strangely, the star north scale of Libra, alias north claw of Scorpio, on this same degree of 'Serpentis' is associated with high intelligence in us, and we shall have an idea why very shortly . . .

The remnants of life that survived the catastrophe – the very word means loss of a star, as also does the word disaster – suffered a cancerous outgrowth of the brain material with the result that a new brain system, only poorly connected to the old one, was created. The old brain is what we now call the cerebellum, whose functioning is still only sketchily understood by today's experts in neurology, while the new growth includes all of the much larger structure, midbrain, hypothalamus, neo-cortex – all that we now speak of as being 'The Brain', assuming as we do that the old cerebellum just runs the automatic workings in us . . .

Ante-Diluvian man's nervous system and intelligence had its center in the cerebellum, the highly efficient brain at the base of our skull whose functions we little understand today. There is no doubt, however, that apart from managing much of our seemingly automatic body workings, it also manages our psychic functioning – not just the remarkable ESP which some people manifest, but also the state we all find ourselves in at times when we just seem to *know* what to do, or how it is going to be, without having calculated it or being taught it through the cerebral cortex.

In common with other creatures, he had only the cerebellum as the summit of the nervous system, and shared a common psychic awareness with all other animal life around him. To have told him this would have been meaningless to him, for he knew of no other state in which one could be. He would not have thought about God as Something or Someone with whom he should seek contact; not having evolved a separated cortex, he knew nothing of 'sin' – that state of lonely separation from the Source of Life.

Dr. Morse points out, moreover, that the origin of the word *sin* has nothing to do with the guilt now associated with it, but comes from an ancient word meaning to be separated or cut off: 'The Irish Political Party, Sinn Féin derives its name from the same root as Sin and was of course formed to gain independence for Ireland from Britain. Mount Sinai likewise derives its name from its cut off position in the desert.'

As Dr. Morse sees it, the 'old brain' goes back to the time when there was an innate bond between all living creatures and a natural sense of connectedness with the Whole, the Source of our being, which the 'new brain' has come to see as a 'God' that is separate from and above us. This 'new brain', in particular its left hemisphere, is that rational, logical part of us which has driven us forward so rapidly in our material evolution and which, as Dr. Morse finally concludes, has, in modern man, little or no communication and interchange with the 'old brain', which we would in today's language define as being the intuitive or even psychic part of us.

Dr. Morse concludes:

> We can now see that what our religions call Sin, (implying in the same breath that it is our personal fault, and for which we shall be condemned unless we repent and behave according to their prescribed dogmas for our salvation), is precisely and only that state of separation, of cut-offness, of almost no clear and intelligible contact between that original brain that we call the Cerebellum and the more recent outgrowth that we call the Cortex, or just 'The Brain'. I cannot say that I have yet seen any religion teach this actual truth of the situation.

Now, as I have mentioned, it is immaterial to me whether you take this interpretation of events literally or choose to see it as another aspect of mythology which gives an insight into the human psyche. In either respect, the important thing is that it ties up our evolution with the question of consciousness, and it addresses the origin of the *rational mind* – that spark which, in evolutionary terms, literally catapulted us into the role of the dominant species on this planet and yet simultaneously drew us further and further from the relative sense of Unity, Balance and Harmony which had previously existed.

This separation between the striding forward mentality of material progress associated with the rational mind and that ancient part of us which yearns to return to the Unity and relative 'innocence' of an earlier age lies at the heart of the conflict which exists deep within our psyche and which is mirrored in the disharmony of our modern world. As we go through the various pivotal periods of the evolution of our human consciousness, we shall see how no major stride forward in material and intellectual terms has been achieved without a deep impact upon the inner psyche of man – to the degree that, until a healing takes place on this deep level within our race and within the planet as a whole, any further technological advance will only draw us closer to the absolute collapse of the fabric of our being, right down to the core of our central nervous and endocrine systems which maintain balance within our bodies.

Our consciousness and the balance within our own body, mind and spirit are intricately woven in with the greater Consciousness and Balance within the planet which nurtures us, so that each becomes a reflection of the other. Just as such new diseases as AIDS and Chronic Fatigue Syndrome (M.E.) are appearing and attacking the very systems within our body which are designed to protect us, so is the Earth beginning to manifest imbalances and extreme conditions which threaten our temporary dominion on this planet.

This is nothing new, but the play is now coming to its resolution. It has nothing to do with our having committed 'sins' or having done wrong. Humanity as a whole has quite simply chosen a path which, as with every action, has its consequences. In exploring the limits of our own consciousness, we have gone as far as we can from the elemental connection with the Whole of which we are all part. It is now time to return to Unity with this Whole and bring with it the expanded awareness and knowledge that we have gained from the path of human experience which we as a species have chosen to follow for these thousands of years. We are blessed with the great gift of free will which each individual has the choice to use. If enough individuals make the same choice, that particular chosen path gains a momentum of its own which will move mountains – hence the weakness of the argument of those who say: 'What difference will my thoughts and actions make to the world?'

So, what do I really mean when I write such seemingly vague terms as Unity or the Whole? As I shall be using these words a lot throughout this book, I think that I should at least explain what they mean to me, as every word has a different nuance to each individual person.

When I use such words as the Whole, the Universe, the Source of our Being or God, I mean very much the same thing: the totality of existence. It is immaterial to me whether one sees this in terms of an intangible Creator or the underlying Order behind Life; as far as I am concerned, it is something that cannot be grasped and defined by our rational mind, and therefore all I can do is to follow my intuition, which knows that there is an 'Energy', for want of a better word, which binds everything together.

Unity is my clearest understanding of the infinite connected-ness of the parts of this Whole with each other and with the Whole itself. Love in its purest form is the ultimate human, conscious expression of Unity.

When I use the word Intuition, I am mirroring Dr. Morse's explanation of the cerebellum, in that it means for me that innate connection with the Whole, which the 'rational' mind cannot define. When I use the term Rational, I am equally mirroring Dr. Morse's explanation of the cortex, in that it signifies that part of the human species which has swept us forward in our evolution: the ability to break down and focus on individual aspects of the Whole in a creative way.

The ultimate duality of spirit and matter, one boundless and the other bound within the constraints of material form, manifests within man as the division between intuition, that indefinable part of us which somehow seems to know the whole picture, and the rational, which needs to define and divide up everything within its scope.

If one analyzes today's overtones of the word intuition or instinct, a frequent association is spontaneity. So often, we hear of the 'instinct of a child' or 'a woman's instinct', by which some innate understanding is implied. In human terms, we associate this with depth of feelings or some creative gift – all very vague terms – but what we really mean is something which naturally exists within us, something that is not actually taught.

Our rational powers, on the other hand, are judged on one's ability to assimilate and analyze facts, to absorb and build on what one is taught. Our whole philosophy, our pursuit of progress is a homage to the power of the rational mind. We believe in a universe which is governed by laws of logic that we can understand or that are at least ultimately within our grasp.

In today's world it is the latter which holds sway, with our intuitive perceptions banished to the realms of the subcon-scious – in total contrast with the early days of man when the intuitive connection within him reigned supreme, with the rational, as it were, waiting in the wings to assert its power.

In mankind's early evolution, I prefer to call the rational mind the sequential mind, for, in its initial form, it manifested itself as that simple ability to move forward from one sequence to another, to distinguish and then to absorb an individual detail and build upon it – a process which, once initiated, becomes self-nourishing: with each new link, the sequence moves on inexorably, even if this was only at a snail's pace at the beginning.

Whether you ascribe to the catastrophe theory or whether you see man as slowly evolving from the apes, this ability to move from one sequence to the next remains a root cause of our evolution, even though, in those early days, there would have been barely any signs to point towards the predominance the sequential mind has achieved today, as we forge ahead from one material achievement to another.

Indeed, when we look back to the early beginnings of man, we must not make the mistake of trying to analyze his inner or outer life from our modern rational perspective, as this would immediately make it impossible for us to enter into a world which was primarily built on an intuitive connection with the Whole, rather than a mind which sees the distinction between everything that our senses perceive. It would be falling into the trap of, in Dr. Morse's terms, judging the 'old brain' from the perspective of the 'new brain'.

When we think of the ancient world, we tend to dismiss our ancestors as primitive or uncivilized without appreciating the same grace and dignity that the so-called primitive societies of today could so easily teach us – especially those who are confronted by the rigors of starvation and other physical deprivation.

Part of this dignity arises from the depth and directness of communication which goes far beyond the verbal complexity of our own language – a complexity which can conceal as much as it can communicate. Communication is one of the essences of our evolution and the one which reflects, more than any other aspect of our behavior, the growth of our reliance on our rational powers. As we have refined our intellectual capacity and stripped away the non-rational aspects of our psyche, the meaning of the word communication has, in our modern world, gone far beyond the connotation of free-flowing interaction between people and has even begun to relate to specific technological elements within our narrow vision of 'progress' which have little to do with human relationships.

Our vision of communication today encompasses the world – with news media, travel, satellites and a technology of information which can be used to feed the minds of mankind's new generations. Communications forms the basis of our 'society of reason'. Our beliefs are fed by the information our minds receive from other sources; whether or not we consciously accept or reject it, we still absorb the information. As the distance between cultures and countries becomes smaller, we assimilate more and more, and often become so obsessed with detail that we lose any sense of a greater whole.

Only recently have we on a conscious level become aware of 'body language' in our species, a fundamental means of communicating beyond a verbal language – something ignored for so long because of the subjugation of the physical world by the rational mind. Our ability to express our thoughts in a precise verbal language reduced the need to use our other senses as a means of communication – as we began to rely more on the spoken word, other sources of communication became obsolete and our awareness of them faded.

We can only conjecture about the 'language' of our early ancestors, but few will disagree that theirs was a total sensory communication compared with the spoken word we use today. These expressions, gestures, postures, sounds and whatever other elements of which we are not necessarily aware betrayed the most basic reactions and signals essential for living within a group. Betray is the operative word here, as this was a Universal Language, innately expressed and recognized by any member within a single group.

In our modern world, it would be difficult for us to come to terms with this concept of a universal language. Although two people may speak the same verbal language, they can choose exactly what they wish to communicate; they can even deceive. If we were threatened with the loss of this power, it would strike at the very heart of our lives: our sense of self, of individual freedom to choose.

The very heart of early man was, however, very different.

The survival of the individual was dependent upon the survival of the group, the extended family unit. The group was therefore invested with the power of Universal Authority and the means of binding and transmitting this power was a universal language.

Once again, the concept of a group of 'primitive' men and women being a power unto itself without a rationally expressed belief system is difficult for us to conceive. We tend to see the self, or maybe some external god, as being the driving force behind our existence, but, for early man, the tightly knit, semi-nomadic group was the essential reality. Just as we pick out particular aspects of the world around us as they relate to us as individuals, the focus of nomadic man was the group itself and those elements outside it which were relevant to survival, such as sources of food, shelter, predators, etc. The only cohesive structure he knew was within the group and this structure would have been a hierarchy of experience: those best equipped to ensure the survival of the group exerted the greatest control within it. The means of keeping this structure in place was the universal language.

The Universal Authority of the Group — a term I shall be using quite a lot — exists on what we would see as two levels. On the most basic, physical level, there is the innate understanding that the survival of the individual is dependent on the survival of the group, and this results in spontaneous co-operation within the group. On a less definable level, there is a relationship with the Earth, its subtle energies and its life forms — a relationship which implies a connection with the Universe as a whole, of which the Earth is a microcosm.

Within this Universal Authority of the Group, many features of our modern consciousness do not exist. The most potent symbol of sequential thought is time: the concept of one moment succeeding another, of past, present and future. For nomadic man, just as for the nomadic herds which still exist in our world today, the primary divisions of time were night and day, the seasons. The passing of these could be directly observed by the senses, and, because of their regularity and their effect on survival, they leave an imprint on the behavioral patterns of the group.

Another dominant characteristic of modern man which did not appear in early nomadic man is his fear of death.

Certainly, early man experienced the physical reaction of fear in relation to death, but only in so far as the object of fear could be perceived by the senses, such as the threat of a powerful predator. Fear of death in a modern sense is a preoccupation of the rational, sequential mind that can look into the future and see a beginning and end in all things; it is not within the scope of a mind locked in the present, the day to day business of survival.

Even today, in some so-called 'primitive' societies, death is seen as passing through a veil, as a cause for celebration for a new journey, as opposed to the mourning of an end of a life. This ritual goes as far back in origin as Neanderthal Man, as documented by Joseph Campbell in *Primitive Mythology*.

> The earliest unmistakable evidences of ritual and therewith of mythological thought yet found have been the grave burials of Homo neanderthalensis, a remote predecessor of our own species, whose period is perhaps to be dated as early as 200,000–75,000 B.C. Neanderthal skeletons have been found interred with supplies (suggesting the idea of another life), accompanied by animal sacrifice (wild ox, bison, and wild goat), with attention to an east-west axis (the path of the sun, which is reborn from the same earth in which the dead are placed), in flexed position (as though within the womb), or in sleeping position – in one case with a pillow of chips of flint. Sleep and death, awakening and resurrection, the grave as a return for rebirth; but whether Homo neanderthalensis thought the next awakening would be here again or in some world to come (or even both together) we do not know.*

Indeed, we do not know how ancient man perceived death, but there was always one person within the group who could pass through this veil and return unharmed to give to the group the certainty of a reality behind it. This was the Shaman, a figure whose origin goes back to the earliest history of mankind and who nevertheless still exists and can be seen at work in certain cultures today.

The Shaman was the intermediary between the group

---

*Joseph Campbell, *Primitive Mythology*, Penguin Books, p.67.

and that Whole of which the group was an integral part. He was, as he is today, the focal point of ritual, which, in its purest, earlier form (as opposed to the dessicated or pompous ritual of modern Western religion), forged the group together as a unified force through the power of song and dance, sound and movement. It was he who brought the group into deeper harmony with the Earth and the Universal Energy which lay behind the fertility of the land and the plenty which Nature offered to ensure the group's survival. It was he also who brought and still brings the numinous into the lives of the members of the group.

To this day, Shamans are picked out at an early stage of their lives by the existing Shaman who recognizes in his successor an innate predisposition for the role. In going through their initiation and in the seemingly uncontrollable behavior which their immense power at times unleashes, Shamans are irrevocably cut off from the normal workings of the group and, yet, it is they who shape the destiny of the group through their connection to the elemental powers beyond the perception of the ordinary person. Through his intensity of experience and exploration into the deepest recesses of the psyche, he is released from the constraints of his immediate environment and assumes the function of the catalyst for change and movement within the group.

In the early hunting groups, the Shamanistic ritual was closely linked with the hunt, creating a bond in the spirit world which would ensure a successful conclusion. One of the earliest signs of this ritual can be seen in the famous rock paintings of the Lascaux caves, where the much discussed art was not just a series of pretty pictures, but symbolic and very precise depictions of the encounters the Shaman would experience behind the veil. The total darkness within the cave, and maybe the flickering of a fire reflecting on the walls, the enhanced vibration raised by the intoxicating effect of song and dance, leading to a state of trance, an altered state of consciousness – all would combine to create an environment which eased the transition into another dimension, the dark correlating to the void beyond of a limitless Universe, where man and beast were one.

Within this boundless void, the spirit of the Shaman and of the animal could become as one, so that the role of the hunter and the hunted could be forged together. For, in this ritual, there is the first evidence of the sacred bond of sacrifice between the killer and the victim – a bond which, when unleashed from the binding force of necessity and genuine consecration and respect would burgeon into the wanton mass sacrifices and slayings of later degenerating societies.

Within a group still at one with the earth, the Shaman's link with these currents beyond the other members' perception was a dynamic, constructive force. However, once the structure of society changed with the act of settling and the advent of agriculture, this unpredictable energy gradually would come to be perceived by the resulting larger and more hierarchical groups as a threatening, disruptive force, ultimately to be squashed by the more formalized religious authority of the priesthood.

In the East, the elemental power of the Shaman was transmuted into the yogi, where the individual force was merged into the higher aspects of his consciousness, leading to a state of peace and harmony with the Source. In the West and other cultures, the power of the individual somehow came to be perceived as a threat to the group, so that the male ego in particular had to be curbed at adolescence in puberty rites which exist to this day in certain cultures and where the uncontrollable individual energies, most apparent in the youth's discovery of his sexuality, had to be submitted to the order of the group as a whole.

At a certain stage in Western man's development, the primeval energies of the Shaman became an object of fear. His ability to 'mediate' between the dual worlds of the physical and the 'spiritual' could no longer be trusted and, in settled communities, passed into the hands of a priestly, largely hereditary caste. The physical and inner spiritual journey of the nomad was replaced by a more structured and formalized religion in which the individual was increasingly cut off from the Source by this priesthood. The Universal Authority of the Group, within which there were no secrets and the Shaman shared his experience of the 'other world' with his tribe, was replaced by the authority of an oligarchy which increasingly lost its connection of unity with its people and thereby ultimately with the Source Itself.

So what was the cause of this seemingly abrupt change where not only was the unity of the group undermined by the sequential mind, but also the intuitive connection with the Source was diminished?

Once again, we need to return to the subject of communication, which is closely linked with those two other hallmarks of early man: dexterity and memory. His dexterity or creativity is the most easily traceable through the physical evidence of fossils and remains of tools used for hunting, clothing, cooking, etc., each new discovery spawning another. His ability to create implements arises out of a sequential mind which enables man to link things physically and mentally. Feeding this creativity is communication within the group which must become more complex and linear, as the creative dexterity grows. Once an activity exceeds the simple level which can be passed on through imitation, the spoken language becomes the means of transmitting information and learning, and in doing so, feeds the progress with which they evolve.

Likewise, memory advances at the same pace. Learning one simple act through imitation needs one act of memory; once this one simple act expands into two acts and then successively onwards, memory expands to ensure that learning is retained and then grows to actively pick out specific elements from the well of past experience.

In the early, nomadic stages of our evolution, all these aspects of the sequential mind seem to lead forward in a harmonious manner: it is the rational which pushes mankind forwards, widening the scope of his powers and experience; it is the non-rational, universal mind which binds the group together and ensures the spirit of co-operation which the rational mind requires, at this early stage, in order to be most effective and to benefit the group as a whole.

A world of comparative simplicity with very few distinctions and no external moral code; a microcosm which is a world unto itself, the individual components inseparable from the whole, the richness of which comes from its connection to the elemental energies of the Earth – such must have been the life of the early semi-nomadic hunter/gatherer groups which existed so successfully and barely changed for so long. It was within the framework of this Universal Group that the sequential mind was nurtured and slowly evolved over an extensive period of time, yet this simple framework was in itself the powerful force responsible for keeping the explosive potential of the sequential mind in check. As long as the simple survival needs of the group were the focus of man's existence, the rational achievements of man would unfold at a snail's pace.

However, like a chick within an egg which feeds upon the nutrients within and then breaks through the shell into the freedom of life, the rational mind, by its expansive nature, ultimately had to break out of the constraining force of the environment which nourished it.

This did not happen instantly, but the measure of control which man slowly began to gain over his environment finally moved into a new phase which irrevocably chimed the death knell of the Universal Authority of the Group: the well-documented transformation from a nomadic to a settled existence.

Of course, the domestication of animals and the planting of crops which one associates with this phase were only slowly integrated into the traditional lifestyle of the Near-Eastern groups in question – archaeological evidence points to a gradual addition of these new means of gathering food to the old over the two thousand years up to 5500 B.C. Yet, once these new methods had become firmly established and self-sufficient settlements abounded, the true power of the sequential mind was unleashed.

Until now, I have barely touched on the essential dualism which reflects one of the most profound divisions from unity: that of male and female. It is from this major transition point of mankind putting roots down in settled communities that the male/female dualism begins to lose its earlier, innate sense of balance and harmony, leading to a conflict which culminates, inevitably when we view it from our historical point of view, with the 'victory' of the male. (The extent of this victory is demonstrated by my continuous reference towards 'man' and 'he', for which I apologize, but which I shall continue to do for 'convenience's' sake!)

We have become so accustomed to a male dominated society, (and this is equally so in the East and the West), that it has only been the relatively recent research of archaeologists and anthropologists which has awoken us to the fact that this was not always the case – indeed, far from it.

When we mention the hierarchy within a group, we are conditioned to think of this in very 'male' terms, but this would be a major error when we are considering the simple hunter/gatherer groups which survived without appreciably changing for so long. We only have to look at the earliest pottery found in the first settlements of man to see the preponderance of the female figure and the strong earth/mother power which she represented at the time.

There she is in her naked glory as the earth goddess, while man, in his rites, is always depicted as dressed in ceremonial clothes – a far contrast with that most male of civilizations, Ancient Greece, where the nude male body was glorified in sculptures, while the female figure remained hidden behind folds of traditional garments.

The body of woman was a mystery in itself, as mysterious as the moon which regulated her cycles. Within her body, the seed of man grew; she was the creator of life and she had the power of transformation, from maiden to mother to crone or shape changer, a view of the trinity within woman which was passed down well into the Middle Ages.

How could she not be the focus of the early hunter/gatherer groups? As the men went out to hunt, she remained in the hearth of the temporary home, looking after and molding the children of the family. The food which she collected as the gatherer was a much more reliable, steady source than the more risky, yet more flamboyant catches of the hunt. She was, in the guise of mother, the steadfast core, which bound the group together in a natural way that needed no external controls. She was that connection to the earth with an innate knowledge of its cycles, and of the healing properties of the herbs which grew around her.

As a natural extension of this, woman, with her intimate connection to the Earth Goddess, must have been the predominant force within the early settlements which initially reaped and then learned to plant the crops indigenous to the Near Eastern regions where agriculture first flourished. The image of the Mother Earth was, in all these early settlements, the symbol of productivity, the nurturing womb from which new life would grow, the cycle of death and renewal, the knowledge and trust in a new harvest as the seasons passed from one to another. And, in early mythology, her male consort is the bull – not the superior male deity which appears in later mythology, but one which rules side by side in equality, balance and harmony.

Perhaps this was the Garden of Eden, the female reaper and the male herder living in harmony with each other and with the Earth, existing within the mutually supporting confines of the group. Yet we know that, however long the intrinsic, connected nature of woman predominated within these early groups, it was man who eventually assumed control and holds it to this very day – at least on an external level, for the female energy still rules our subconscious and much more even of our conscious mind than we would dare to admit.

The demise of the binding power of woman within group living* and the rise of man are inextricably linked with the rise of sequential mind. Indeed, the rise of the male and of the sequential mind seem to be indistinguishable, as they both appear to be results of and creators of the same process: the beginning of the dissolution of the Universal Authority of the Group, the separation between man and God, and an emphasis on individual consciousness, which leads to a further separation between man and man, let alone man and woman.

In most ancient mythology, the female energy represents that cohesive force which naturally binds the group together. In her threefold guise of maiden/mother/crone, she represents the eternal cycle of unity, with death seen as a re-entry into the womb for life to begin anew – in evidence in some late Paleolithic tombs, where the dead are buried in the fetal position surrounded by statuettes of the Goddess. Even the Universe itself is sometimes portrayed as being born from the womb of the Great Mother, the dark void from which all things come.

However, in a world of duality where man gradually becomes conscious of self, and, in doing so, feels his separateness from the Source of all Being and from the individuals

---

*This also coincides with the demise of the Shaman as a creative force, for his elemental force was just as much of a threat to the new male hierarchy as was the mysterious, inner power of woman.

within his group, the role of woman takes on a more threatening, frightening aspect. Her threefold, unified nature of maiden, mother, crone now becomes three distinct natures, and the power which each represents is seen as disruptive by a new order that has established its own power on an externally imposed structure, as opposed to the natural order of unity which had previously existed.

As a maiden, she is the focus of man's sexual desire, the one element within himself which is beyond the control of the sequential mind. Spontaneous sexual arousal, just like the ecstatic frenzy of the Shaman, throws off the shackles of any outside force, and, in the case of woman, submits the male energy to the mysteries of female power. Instead of seeing the sexual act as one of union on every level, rational man somehow came to shroud it in guilt and fear.

In the Judeo/Christian/Moslem world, the natural expression of sex, sexuality and the emotions which increasingly arose out of them as man became more self-conscious has come to be perceived as a potentially destructive force which must be controlled within pre-established limits. Instead of seeing sex as a sacred act, our society has debased its vital energies by insisting on it solely as a means of producing offspring, rather than understanding sexuality as a physical expression of our spiritual being.

The realization of the creative/destructive power of sexual energy goes back to the earliest settlements of man. In *Primitive Mythology*, Joseph Campbell describes the rituals of contemporary, primitive cultures which mirror ancient myths from the earliest neolithic planting communities where sex and death go hand in hand in order to create fertility of the land. In a relatively contemporary culture, a young maiden and boy are ritualistically crushed to death in the middle of intercourse, so that destruction can bring forth creation in the form of fertility; in the ancient myths, a serpent (not forgetting its elemental symbology) or a 'divine' being or a maiden is killed, often after sexual union with the 'hero' or 'heroine' of the tribe in question and from their buried body or head grow the first food-bearing plants.

This link between sex and death and fertility is exclusive to the primitive planting communities, and signals the early stages of the awareness of duality, where life and death, male and female have become separate realities, cut off from a sense of unity with the Source. The sacrifices mentioned above, whether in reality or in myth, are not just primitive blood-letting; they are an attempt, by a mind where the distinction between unity and duality is still blurred, to re-enact, though ritual, the continuous cycle of death and rebirth. This is, in a sense, the essence of ritual in modern times: to take man beyond his rational perspective, where everything must be proved, to an intuitive space which connects with the Source – yet, in such cases of human sacrifice, a sense of separateness has come to exist, whereby human lives must be offered to an *External Source*, rather than *trusting* in a group's innate connection to the Whole.

Within this same mentality of separateness, the second aspect of woman, the mother figure, so closely linked to the nurturing, unifying aspect of Mother Earth, also becomes a symbol of awe and fear. The very act of birth, of emerging from the dark, comforting void of the womb into the dazzling light of day is a traumatic event within the psyche of man, an actual physical separation completed with the cutting of the umbilical cord. This physical separation is analogous to Jung's 'psychic birth' of man – away from the comforting, familiar unity of the group into the primeval jungle of individual experience and the expansive light of consciousness which comes to a finite end with the 'darkness' of death.

So it is that, as the sequential mind develops, the female goddess assumes the dual nature of birth and death, the mother and the death crone, nourishing and destructive – no longer a symbol of the eternal cycle of life, but an object of fear to the dualistic mind which gradually embraces the material, finite view of death. For it is in the material world that the Universal Authority of the Group finally begins to crumble and the dualistic mind takes hold, creating a final separation from the Source and yet opening up mankind to a growth and expansion which to this day may seem boundless.

The relative reliability of food sources within these settled communities and the comparative ease of life which resulted from this had two major consequences which have continued unabated to this present moment in our evolution: the growth of population and of possessions. Both of these are inextricably linked and served as a catalyst for the growing supremacy of the sequential mind over the intuitive nature which was the hallmark of early man.

In nomadic life, possessions were an encumbrance. No group constantly on the move could afford to carry more than bare necessities. However, when man settled, such limitations on possessions were eliminated and, indeed, the objects, food and tools that man accumulated around him served as an integral part of his survival, an insurance for the future. Furthermore, the sequential mind which had for so long been limited to inventing a few rudimentary tools was suddenly released from the constraints imposed by the single minded struggle of nomadic existence and burst forth in a surge of creative energy. The simplest of inventions needed to domesticate plant and animal life spawned further inventions, and each new discovery led to a gradual sophistication of tools and machines which harnessed the power of nature. From this point on, the evolution of mankind and the manipulation of his environment are inextricably linked.

Within this changing balance of life, old roles inevitably changed and the old structure which naturally bound together the early, small hunter gatherer culture gradually crumbled to be replaced by a new order. As population grew, as verbal language and the division of labor became more complex, differences between the individuals within a group would begin to be ingrained within man's consciousness – the consciousness of self which drives man further away from the Universal Consciousness, the Unity of his ancestors.

Much has been written about the so-called 'selfish' nature of man, but the self-interest which is inherent within all of us is no more than an extension of the survival instinct of the hunter/gatherer group. When the Universal Authority is invested within the group, all relates to the survival of the group; when this Authority crumbles and is transferred to a family circle and then increasingly to the individual, the survival instinct evolves into family- or self-interest. This is a natural evolutionary process; the negative association we feel towards the term self-interest arises from the opposite state of the Universal Authority of the Group, when self-interest is not counterbalanced by an inherent feeling for the larger group of humanity.

We must remember that the earliest settlements probably numbered no more than 200 people – more, perhaps, than a typical semi-nomadic extended family unit, but still not enough for a major hierarchical structure of power to come into being. However, as the sequential, rational mind took hold and man began to control his environment, there is no doubt that a certain specialization within groups would occur, whereby certain tasks would be fulfilled by certain individuals.

Within a nomadic group bound by the Universal Authority of the Group, each person's activities were bound most probably by sex and by age, by what they were physically most suited to do. Within this fluid structure, those who contributed most to the welfare of the group would doubtless direct the energies of the group, but this was only a temporary leadership as physical power fades with age.

Whereas 'natural selection' ensures that only the fittest survive, thereby creating a certain equality within a single species evolving in the same environment, man's ability to control his environment is not subject to such simple laws. 'Intelligence' – that ability to put sequential thoughts together to create a new reality – is a much more random phenomenon. This ability to assimilate and build on information handed down from one generation to another seems to vary from one individual to another, from one cultural region to another. The world of the rational mind is a world of inequality and of widening gaps, because, unlike physical domination which fades and is replaced with new blood, the power created by intelligence can be handed down and built on within each generation of a specific unit. With the growth of self-interest following the fading of the Universal Authority of the Group, and with the greater separation caused by population growth and increasingly extended family units, this inequality grows until it becomes institutionalized in the first city-states which appeared around 3500 B.C.

Possessions are an important adjunct of intelligence. First of all, they are a result of man's creative mind, and, at the same time, they delineate inequality in easily perceivable terms. From the moment man settles in one place, begins to build houses and accumulate things around him, possessions become the symbol of success and of power. If we combine this with the inequality created by intelligence, as well as the innate drive within man to improve his material condition and the competition created by man's increasing population, the perpetual conflict which is the hallmark of our history can be seen as an understandable progression in our evolution. As the spiritual, unified essence of man's being fades, the temporal, material world takes over and possession becomes the stimulus for and the reward of power.

The need to create an external order, a system of government arises out of this conflict, but, even in its simplest beginnings, government has an inherent duality. A governing class is one which has used its intelligence and strength to elevate itself above the governed class – an action ruled by self-interest. Government is perceived as necessary to create order, to harness man's energy and to prevent futile conflict and bloodshed – this action is for the good of the extended group, and in particular for the good of the governing class! Once the Universal Authority of the Group crumbled and the feeling of connection to the natural order of things was lost, the essence of external government has increasingly become the maintenance of a status quo for the governing class and a drive for material progress, ultimately at the expense of the spiritual essence of mankind. There is nothing inherently right or wrong in this process; it is, quite simply, a natural progression from the growth of the sequential mind within the environment which nurtured this growth.

The pace of this change was not, of course, as brisk as I may make it appear. There were about 2000 years between the initial agricultural settlements and the first-city states in Sumeria, Harappa and Egypt; and, even beyond this period, the sequential mind did not completely destroy man's connection to the Earth and the Universe.

However, it was the perception of this connection which changed. In the hunter/gatherer semi-nomadic groups, the connection was innate within the group. What is difficult for modern man to conceive is that the senses of nomadic man were attuned to elements within the Earth now beyond our perception, such as 'nature spirits' which were connected to certain shrines located along the well-trodden path of their annual migrations and associated with different seasons, climates and therefore patterns in their lives.

This innate knowledge of the cycles of Nature created a ritual out of the nomadic journey itself, in which well-trodden paths were followed, no doubt fixed within the collective memory of the group. The Walkabout, sporadically undertaken by Australian Aborigines in which they follow the ancient, sacred paths of their ancestors, is a modern example of this journey. These paths are full of sites which emit an elemental energy and vibration which can only be felt by a race, such as the Aborigines, which has never severed its connection to the Earth. For them, as with early nomadic man, the outer journey is inseparable from the inner journey, something that Western man has only ever managed to recreate in mythic form such as in the medieval Quest for the Holy Grail.

When man settled, this sacred element of his nomadic journey was lost forever and was replaced by a more formalized spiritual experience based on organized ritual which was created by man around the passing of the seasons to relive in some way the lost unity of his physical/spiritual journey.

There was, within man, an inherent loss in the act of settling – the rituals I have mentioned in which death must always precede life are a sign of the deep psychological impact of such a transition. This need for a formalized ritual, whether it involved sex, sacrifice or some other means of connecting with or appeasing the spirit of the Earth and the Universe, was the beginning of religion as we know it: looking back to and attempting to recreate, in however transitory and artificial a form, the mythic 'Golden Age' of unity and harmony. And yet, as the sequential mind forged onwards, even the religious experience was merged with the need to understand and conceptualize, and the intuitive thread which was the true connection to the Source wore thinner and thinner.

Thus it is that the sequential mind, even in its early development, drew mankind gradually away from Unity with the Whole. The results of its increasing predominance and the subsequent waning of the Universal Authority of the Group were there to see even in the earliest civilizations: the gradual dawning of individual consciousness and the inequality which ultimately arose from the distinctions it made, from the growth of population and material possessions – all establishing a basis for the evolution of modern man.

From our modern perspective, it can be very easy to

look at these aspects of our evolution in a negative light. We can see individual consciousness in terms of 'ego', which we can in turn judge as being the root of selfishness, pride, competitiveness and intolerance; we can see inequality in terms of exploitation of the weak by the powerful, of the poor by the rich; we can see the pollution and terrible state of our environment as being the result of our obsession with material prosperity at all costs.

What we must understand, though, is that these negative associations have arisen quite simply because these aspects of our evolution have not been nurtured within an environment where the connection between all beings and the Whole is innately felt. Our awareness of self is what enables us to expand our experience and consciousness, so that we may use our free will to act with responsibility and individual conscience; inequality is part of the diversity of such a world and our responsibility is to use our individual talents for the good of the Whole; our material achievements are a result of great human creativity, and our responsibility is in not allowing destruction to be a result of this creativity.

When we unfavorably judge the results of the 'triumph' of the sequential mind, we not only miss the point, but we are also using our own energy in an uncreative way. It is only by understanding how we have allowed this powerful element of the human make-up to create disharmony in our world that we can get to the root of the ills of our society and start to build a new vision of Unity.

Chapter 3

Man and God

When one considers the relatively simultaneous emergence of the great city-states of Sumeria, Egypt, Harappa and Crete, one genuinely begins to wonder whether early man did at this point in time come into contact with some higher life form or consciousness which suddenly propelled him faster along the path of evolution towards becoming the rational beings we are now. Can 'normal' evolutionary theory really account for the seemingly instant appearance all at one time of writing, mathematics, astronomy, architecture on a grand scale, the wheel, a system of taxation, to name but a few?!

The accepted viewpoint is that these all began in Sumeria in the fertile valleys of the Euphrates and Tigris rivers, and then spread through trade to Harappa in the Indus valley in what is now Pakistan and to Egypt and then to Crete. Yet, Harappa, with its grid-like city plan, and Egypt, with its distinctive culture and edifices, were nothing like the spread out Sumerian cities. Were these distinct styles due simply to geographical or climatic differences, or were there other forces at work? There are many unanswered questions.

What is certain, though, is that the inequality which is the hallmark of our civilization becomes institutionalized in this stage of man's development. The original unity within a single harmonious group has now splintered up into very distinct hierarchies – a structure of imposed order which endured in varying degrees of rigid application well into the Middle Ages. Such distinctions are a reflection of the fundamental dualism of the intuitive nature of man which is connected to the Whole, and the rational nature of man which divides his world into individual parts which he can comprehend with his sequential mind. No longer is there the intimate relationship with the Universe and the immediate environment of the Earth which fulfills the needs of the group; now, a different relationship has developed, whereby a new priestly caste has arisen to act as an intermediary between the Whole and the individual people living within Its embrace.

Within the first city-states, this division between the macrocosm of the Whole and the microcosm of the individual community was evident in the different way that the female goddess had come to be perceived. This process is charted by Joseph Campbell in his *Occidental Mythology*:

Now in the neolithic village stage of this development and dispersal, the focal figure of all mythology and worship was the bountiful goddess Earth, as the mother and nourisher of life and receiver of the dead for rebirth. In the earliest period of her cult (perhaps c. 7500–3500 B.C. in the Levant) such a mother goddess may have been thought of only as a local patroness of fertility, as many anthropologists suppose. However, in the temples even of the first of the higher civilizations (Sumer, c. 3500–2500 B.C.), the Great Goddess of highest concern was certainly much more than that. She was already, as she is now in the Orient, a metaphysical symbol: the arch personification of the power of Space, Time and Matter, within whose bound all being arise and die: the substance of their bodies, configurator of their lives and thoughts, and receiver of their dead. And everything having form or name – including God personified as good or evil, merciful or wrathful – was her child, within her womb.*

---

*Joseph Campbell, *Occidental Mythology*, Penguin Books, p.7.

The essence of this fundamental shift in focus from the intimate connection to the Earth to the grander scale of the Cosmos is the beginning of conceptual thinking. That same rational mind, which created the structure of the cities themselves and all the inventions mentioned at the beginning of this chapter, was also responsible for this new view of the world in which the Universe was perceived in relation to human experience and comprehension. Instead of just feeling a natural sense of connection to the Earth, this new type of man now needed to establish an outer order — one which was reflected in the celestial order of the night sky, of the 'fixed' stars and the planets revolving through the Cosmos in measurable cycles.

The representation of this cyclical view of the Universe, of a cosmic order beyond the control of man, was Woman, manifesting her own mysterious cycles as the Great Goddess, the expansive, infinite void without shape or form. Yet, somewhere along the path of evolution of these cities, the female influence diminished and the new hierarchy of power came to be dominated by men and by the rational mind. The first stage of separation away from the natural connection with the Whole and towards a more conceptual view of this same Whole lay the groundwork for 'formalized religion' as we know it, where man, as opposed to woman, became the interpreter of Its mysteries — to the point that even the Great Goddess of infinite mystery was ultimately supplanted in most Western cultures by a male God or gods, endowed with human, (often unsavory!), characteristics.

Again and again, one comes back to this continuous link between the rational mind, the left side of the brain and the male sex on the one hand and the intuitive mind, the right side of the brain and the female sex on the other. Why this should be so is another of the hidden secrets of the evolution of our species, yet, from the earliest mythology onwards, the female symbolizes the expansive nature of the Universe beyond the rational understanding of man, whilst the male is all which gives form to the world around us and divides this limitless Universe into parts to which we can relate. Neither one nor the other is superior, as they are both aspects of being, but, right up to this present day, the rational and male have succeeded in combining to create a supremacy which has ultimately suppressed the intuitive and female. In the West, we have chosen to see the male and rational as being the primary, active principle in our society, with the female, creative energy relegated to a secondary, supporting role – and, in doing so, we have created a society of division and indifference to the condition of the one's fellow beings, rather than one of Unity and compassion.

If one sees man and the Universe joined together as one, then the division of man into two – the creation of the bicameral mind and the dawning of consciousness – results in the release of an immensely powerful energy. In reality, it signifies an expansion of the Universe itself and the impact of this division is far greater than anything our rational minds can conceive of, such as the splitting of an atom.

Psychologically, this release of energy was like a shock wave reverberating through the essential being of mankind, and, however slowly this may seem to have occurred through our perception of linear time, it was, in evolutionary terms, a sudden transformation which created a lasting, traumatic effect: the duality of, on the one hand, the fear engendered by the 'loneliness' of separation from and the subconscious longing to return to the Source, and, on the other hand, the struggle of the conscious mind to follow its innate drive forwards to explore and create the 'best' reality on the physical plane.

Early 'conscious' man must have been pulled in so many directions, not least by those strange companions of consciousness: our emotions. Deeply imprinted within the human psyche were those nebulous feelings of fear following this 'fall from Unity' and of guilt that we did something wrong to deserve this fall – so inextricably were these emotions linked with the process of separation from the Source that the new separate 'God' created by the minds of man became an angry Superbeing to be appeased because He had punished us by banishing us to this new imperfect world where we were at His mercy. To this day, such fear and lack of self-worth linger deep within the psyche of Western man.

Not only do we now find the separation between man and God, but there also develops a separation between man and man – where the priestly caste of these structured cities, now seeing harmony with the Universe in increasingly mathematical terms based on astronomy, came to act as an intermediary between this God and the 'common' man. Initially, male and female may well have shared the sacred rites entrusted to this priesthood, but, even when this Higher Being was still acknowledged as the Great Goddess, it was the male who eventually prevailed, acting as the authority which brought form and understanding to the formless infinity of the Universe.

Even within these divisions, there arose one more division at the peak of this hierarchy: that of the mystical, spiritual power of the priesthood and the temporal, material power of the kingship. In the early days of the city-states, it was the former which held sway over the latter, for the king was with regularity ritually sacrificed by the priesthood according to specific cycles interpreted through the positions of the stars and planets in the night sky.

This action, which seems perverse to modern man, was, in these new more populous and structured civilizations, an external means of creating the continuous renewal of leadership on the physical plane which had happened naturally in earlier, smaller, semi-nomadic groups. Just as the Shaman in earlier times had initiated a ritual to create a bond of accord between hunter and hunted, this 'immolation' of the king was a process whereby the slayer and the victim worked in accord as one in order to re-enact the divine principle of eternal renewal for the benefit of the group as a whole – in the belief that, with the death of the old king and the accession of the new, the energy of the group would be revitalized and its link to the Earth would be re-established in greater plenty.

Of course, our modern consciousness cannot help being somewhat appalled by the need for bloodshed to create renewal, for there appears to be only a short step before this degenerates into the kind of mass sacrifice in evidence in the Inca and Aztec cultures at the time of the Spanish conquests. However, as I have said before, we cannot judge such acts from our modern standpoint, particularly with a mentality which sees life and death in finite terms.

On the other hand, it is evident that the necessity of such ritual sacrifice points to a crisis point of duality in the evolution of mankind. There is obviously still an ingrained memory of the old way of life ruled by the natural cycles of the Earth, but the sequential mind has advanced too far for it to return to the simple existence which initially nourished it. In this transition point where the Universal Authority of the Group has still not completely vanished, but where man is becoming increasingly aware of his individual needs, the immolation of the king by the priesthood represents a final attempt to preserve the supremacy of the spiritual Unity of the Whole over the material world of separation.

However, the very process of one controlling the other is in itself another step away from Unity – it is as if the spirit, in being divorced from the material plane, has been cut off from the source of its true vital force. From this point on, one can begin to envisage the scenario of a degenerating culture. Where the sense of unity within the group begins to fade as the increasing population and prosperity create divisions into specialists such as priests, merchants, peasants, etc., the self-aware individuals at the peak of the hierarchy find themselves with unlimited scope to use their power for their own ends. Even though the priesthood no doubt began with an innate sense of connection with and then responsibility to the group, its increasing remoteness from the masses combined with its loss of connection to the Earth would lead it eventually to an awareness of its own special position of power and the natural desire not to surrender any aspect of it, especially the material security and comfort.

This is a natural progression of awareness of self, which would occur first at the peak of the hierarchy. When the material world of possessions enters into the fray, the desire to hold on to the physical rewards of power and the resulting fear of losing them stimulates the need to control and create the institution of government from above. We know that the sacrifice of kings within the early cultures faded away and the material and spiritual ultimately became joined together as one – not the old unity based on the welfare of the group, but a new ruling class in which the spiritual was engulfed by the material.

Within this new order, the central spiritual authority also faded. With the rise of individual consciousness gradually filtering through to the masses, a degenerate priesthood could not sustain a unified concept of the Godhead, as each individual would need his own 'religious' experience. This may have initially been provided by mass ceremony, such as we still see to this day, but archaeological evidence shows that, at about this time, images of personalized gods, representing individual facets of consciousness, were common in the homes of ordinary people.

The Universal Authority of the Group is now in its death throes, and it is the creative/destructive force of the individual ego which is now unleashed in this new world of duality. This is the force which I believe to be responsible for the simultaneous crumbling of the great city-states in the middle of the second millennium B.C., for an external, artificial authority, still looking back to and often trying to recreate the past, more concerned with its own power than with the welfare of its subjects, did not have the ability to keep in check the mass of individual energies which had been released from the natural constraints of the Universal Authority of the Group.

The civilizations of Crete and Harappa completely disappeared, Sumeria was overrun by warlike, nomadic folk, as was Egypt for a while. The most obvious cause is the coming of the Iron Age and the appearance of these heavily armed tribes smashing their way through the more passive, unarmed cities. Yet, if these cities were at the peak of their civilization, would they have so easily succumbed with all the intelligence they had at hand? Or, just as happened thousands of years later in Central and South America, had these civilizations declined and become so rotten from inside that any band of marauders could have swept them aside?

The internal collapse of these early civilizations is easy to comprehend. As the awareness of every individual within the hierarchy becomes stronger, the means by which the ruling class is able to maintain its superiority must depend more on control, and, as has been seen throughout history including our contemporary world, the end result is eventually always the same: the ultimate breakdown of the old order, opening the gates for a new structure of power to come flooding in.

In a sense, the final, total collapse of the Universal Authority of the Group had exactly the same effect that the fall of all governments would have in modern times: Chaos. The mass of individual egos devoid of all control, whether internal or external, wipe away the structures of the old, and only after a 'Dark Age' of constant flux and chaos, such as appears in regular cycles from this point on in human history, does a new order gradually form out of the remnants of the old.

From this point on, also, the Unity of the group was to be superseded by the rise of the individual. However many controls successive ruling powers may have tried to impose on the energy of the individual ego, they have merely been transient efforts to put the lid back on Pandora's box. From these early civilizations to this very day, individual consciousness has been continuously striving to break free from the constraints of hierarchical power. Since the breakdown of the Universal Authority of the Group, history has shown one oligarchy after another imposing more and more rigid controls because they fear the elemental energies of the individual as being destructive and a threat to their own power.

Little do they understand that each individual is part of an eternal cycle which lies far beyond their control and which must, in its own time and its own way, follow the path which ultimately leads back to Unity.

Chapter 4

Egypt and the Decline of a Civilization

While the original area of the Sumerian cities in Mesopotamia became engulfed in constant war, and the cities of Crete and Harappa quite literally crumbled, the great enclosed state of Egypt seemed to be a relative haven of peace and stability. However, this was an illusion, as the same disintegration which had weakened the other civilizations was simultaneously taking place within this amazing culture. It was only the protection afforded by its geographical position and the rigid structure within the society itself which permitted Egypt to continue an unbroken, albeit somewhat sporadic, tradition — even beyond its occupation by Rome.

The history of Egyptian civilization is one of a sudden rise to incredible heights from what appeared to be virtually nothing, followed by a steady decline, the cause of which differs very little from the root of the collapse of the other city-states. We are fortunate in that the insularity, the strong oral tradition and the monumental structures left behind by this great civilization have allowed modern man to build an impression of its history. It is only sad that most Egyptologists have chosen to view it, with all its diversity and complexity, through very materialistic and simplistic modern eyes. What most of them have failed to comprehend is the extent to which the Egyptian's view of the Cosmos, the Source of All Being to which all living beings ultimately return, infused every aspect of his life, personal or public.

Also, there has been little questioning as to how such an advanced civilization sprang up overnight in evolutionary terms. Out of crude neolithic cultures, there evolved what is now referred to as the Pre-Dynastic* period which culminated in the military unification of the reputedly two rival states of northern and southern Egypt by the legendary Menes, supposedly in 3050 B.C. Whether this is exact historical fact is open to conjecture, especially as no written history of Egypt appeared until the 3rd century B.C. It has even been suggested that this unification may be of a more symbolic significance as a representation of the highest point of Unity within the civilization, from which a further division into duality subsequently occurred.

Whether the unification was historical or symbolic, the fact remains that this point in time marks the seemingly instantaneous appearance of those same elements of high culture that we saw in the early Sumerian cities, such as writing, astronomy, mathematics, etc. In Pre-Dynastic remains which have hitherto been unearthed, there was no evidence of such a thing as writing, yet, when they did appear, the hieroglyphs which we associate with ancient Egypt did not seem to slowly evolve; they immediately existed in their complete form.

Given such evidence, it would seem presumptuous to dismiss the idea that the indigenous population of the region came into contact with some higher race or civilization which initiated the sudden flowering of this extraordinary culture.

What is sure is that, at this early height of dazzling achievement, there existed certain beliefs and structures which have become the hallmark of Egyptian civilization: a Pharaoh at the apex of the hierarchical pyramid embodying the Source of All Being in physical form; a lesser hierarchy of priests, merchants, peasants; a panoply of gods, each a manifestation of an aspect of the Whole; monumental structures built on the universal principles of mathematics. And, unifying all these

---

*Little survives of this period, except archaeological evidence of underground tombs and highly adorned ceremonial ornaments found within them.

aspects, temporal or eternal, material or spiritual, is the cosmic ordering principle without which even the gods are powerless to act: 'Maat', the female, all-encompassing principle of order comparable to the natural Unity of the group, but here given, for the first time, a name, thereby becoming a concept, an adjunct of rational thought – albeit immeasurable, indefinable, just like the Indian concept of 'dharma', that force which binds the Universe together.

In this early 'dynastic' world after the unification of Egypt, it is Maat which reigns supreme, embodied in the famous Narmer Palette of c. 2850 B.C. as the cow-goddess Hathor whose four heads tower over even the sun principle of the falcon and the striding figure of the pharaoh. In later Dynasties, Hathor is relegated to become a secondary goddess of childbirth and healing, yet, in this early period, She is the cosmic womb from whose milk the pharaoh receives nourishment. The Pharaoh as a principle is the spirit of Unity, bringing order out of primordial chaos; the pharaoh as a man is the earthly embodiment of this principle and is beholden to the community which he governs.

The incredible diversity of gods under this cosmic principle of Maat is a reflection of the imagination and resulting symbolism which emerged from the growing rational nature of man. In a mind which is primarily in unity with the Source, it is the fusion with the active principle of the rational side which gives man's creative power the impetus to relate aspects of the Source to individual experience. (The other end of the spectrum of 'Imagination' is in our modern world, where the rational mind reigns supreme and where the great creative minds and artists of our day are able to step back from a linear mode of thinking and connect with the more 'instinctive' well of knowledge and sensation which lies behind the veil of our material existence.)

This is the essence of the glorious symbolism of the hieroglyphs – a form of writing quite unlike our literal language with its precise meaning. The grammatical language of hieroglyphic writing is quite subsidiary to the symbolism which appeals to the many levels of human consciousness that exist alongside the intellect. It is certainly the language of the few, of the hierarchy which created its form; but it is also the language of the common man, in that the Universal Principles which it depicts strike a chord in each individual being, evoking an awareness of a reality beyond physical perception and bringing innate knowledge into the outer world of experience.

However elitist religion may have been in Egypt with the most important sacred rites performed in secret by the priesthood, the animal symbolism of the gods brings a spiritual connection into the realm of all men and women – not unlike the animal spirits of Native American tradition.

My favorite of all is the god Khepri, the scarab beetle which is seen again and again on the inscriptions within the tombs and in the Book of the Dead, embodying the divine principle of transformation: from eggs (representing spiritual potential) being laid into a ball of dung (representing matter) which is rolled by the mother along her path for 40 days while, inside, the egg transforms into a larva and a nymph before finally emerging into the light of day as a winged (spiritual) creature. This is god as a pure symbol, as a representation of a divine principle, as opposed to the gods with human personality which we shall see in later Greek myths.

This duality between spirit and matter, embodied in Khepri, strongly pervades every aspect of Egyptian life, as does the recurring theme of divine potential within all mortal beings. It is the act of Consciousness incorporating into Matter which is the very act of Creation – from which point, the consciousness in matter (i.e. the physical, living, human being) always looks to the Source until it makes the transition into death, thereby returning to the Source.

The Pharaoh is the living symbol of this principle. The Pharaoh never dies. When the pharaoh, the individual man, dies, he goes on a journey in a boat to the Underworld – a journey to his next life – often accompanied by his close family who choose to follow him, as death, being a passing through a veil, holds no fears. The process of death is one of unity, of transformation from the confined world of matter to the freedom of spirit, where a man's 'ka' (his individual essence) is united with his 'ba' (his divine, eternal spirit).

Following the union of the two Egypts, the first structured hierarchy of the gods created by the mind of man came into being. The indeterminate, spacious principle of Maat was replaced at the head by Re, the solar principle behind all creation, in its manifestation as Re-Atum, the first male god known to rule over creation.

It is as if this union of the country by fire and arms was symbolic of the dawning of male predominance, the active principle of the sun, rather than the cyclical energy of the moon. However, even with this new force, the gods spawned by Re-Atum and therefore his underlying principle were in themselves part of a cycle. For Re was created through the process of masturbation out of Nun, the primordial state, and from there produced the sacred nine gods, (the Heliopolitan Ennead), including Isis and Osiris, who, in later times, were themselves worshipped as the divine principle.

The myth of Osiris, Isis, Horus and Set is probably the most famous of all Egyptian myths and is worth retelling as it has within it many of the most important elements not only of Egyptian thought, but also of the mystery of unity into duality creating a trinity far clearer than and certainly antecedent to the confused trinity of formalized Christianity.

The story, as handed down in fragments, goes very much like this. The god Geb transfers his powers to Osiris who co-rules Earth with his sister-wife Isis. Osiris is responsible for passing the knowledge of agriculture and of all the high arts to humanity. However, his brother Set becomes jealous of him and resolves to destroy him. At a feast, Set entices Osiris into a chest, locks him up and casts it into the river. Isis, on finding out about this, enters upon a search for the chest, which she ultimately finds hidden in the trunk of a tree which has been made into a pillar for a king's palace. She brings the chest home to Egypt, but, once again, Set manages to get hold of the body of Osiris, which, this time, he cuts up into 14 pieces, scattering them throughout the land. After another quest, Isis finds all the different parts of Osiris's body with the exception of the phallus, which Set had thrown into the river where it had been eaten by a fish. Isis embalms the remaining pieces of the body, creating the first mummy. Meanwhile, she gives birth to a son by Osiris called Horus, who, upon reaching manhood, fights and overcomes Set.However, in the many myths involving Horus and Set, Set is never destroyed and the two are ultimately reconciled. Osiris returns from the Underworld, transfers his earthly powers to Horus and retires to the kingdom of the gods.

This story is rife with symbolism – the four main protagonists, both individually and in their interaction with each other, point us towards a greater understanding of the motivation behind Egyptian life and thought.

Osiris begins as the divine in mortal form. His double death and the splitting up of his body followed by his re-incarnation represents the eternal cycle of regeneration which every person must undergo. He must pass through levels of separation from the Unity of the Cosmos and achieve the ultimate expansion of consciousness through the trials of human experience, before he can integrate his 'ka', his individual being, with his 'ba', the animating principle behind his being, in one last creation, and then finally transcend the transitory, mortal form.

So, he is the living symbol for all mortals, within each of whom is the spark of the divine to be nurtured and to grow on the journey towards enlightenment. It is no wonder that, as the human aspect of the gods became more concrete in the later dynasties of Egypt, Osiris became the most widely syncretized of all: as the 'vegetal' god of the cycles of the earth; as the god of death and resurrection, judging the dead alongside Maat, who became the goddess of cosmic order and harmony. He was usually depicted as bearing the Shepherd's Crook (the Shepherd of mankind), the Flail (sepa-rating the wheat from the chaff) and the 'Was' (the scepter of dominion) – having been through his own transformation, he was the symbol of a benevolent, omniscient power, guiding his flock through their own inner transformation.

Just as Osiris could be the personification of all men, Isis is the personification of woman, in her guise as the Great Goddess, that female, creative power which conceives all living creatures. In her devotion to life, she is the one continuous thread throughout the myth, carrying the seed of the dead and resurrected god and giving birth to the realized divine principle. She is the one calm power untouched by the jealousies and rivalries of man.

Horus is not just the realized divine principle within this myth, but is also thus numerologically. Not only does he complete the Osiris-Isis-Horus triad, but, after the nine of the Ennead, is the tenth god, which, reduced in numerological terms, is One, Unity – not the original Unity of being, but, through the experience of mortal striving, is an expansion of the Unity from which it originally came.

Just as important as Horus to this second greater Unity is Set, without whom the original Unity could not have been expanded. He is a great, creative god, as, without his opposition to unity and order, there could be no creation. Creation needs an opposing force of resistance and a motivating principle to exist and therefore Set is the personification of Duality, the 'dark' force of disharmony, through the integration of which harmony on a greater scale can be attained.

He is, of course, the ancestor of the Christian Satan, and the different ways in which Set and Satan are perceived underline the fundamental straying of Christian teaching. Satan is a dark force which must be repelled and destroyed, while Set is a dark destructive/creative force which must be *reconciled* with the light of Horus. The modern suppression of our 'dark side' lies at the root of the imbalance of our Western society, for it cuts off a return to Unity.

This is one of the great lessons which still has to be learned by us all in today's world and which I shall expand upon in the second half of this book. As we have gone through our evolution into the dualistic beings we have become, separated from the Unity with the Whole, we have judged and thereby cut off certain aspects of our being, and, in doing so, we have allowed them to create an energy of their own which leads even further from Unity. This is what the 'dark side' or what our modern judgmental nature chooses to call 'evil' is all about. In separating ourselves from those aspects of our being which we term 'evil' or 'sin', as opposed to understanding them as part of our human nature and reconciling them into our being, we imbue them with a 'dark', negative energy which increases their power over us.

The myth of Osiris therefore illustrates the essence of the Egyptian belief of Unity expanding into Duality through experience and conflict and returning to the Source as a greater Unity by the assimilation of the dark, shadow side – a belief shared by the early Christian gnostics who were so brutally suppressed as heretics by the Church establishment. Within the Egyptian and gnostic world, the richness of life is to be experienced through the free will of individual experience: in the Christian ethic, the individual spiritual journey is perceived as a threat, and behavior beyond prescribed limits is given the label of 'evil', as if evil is something which is created by some outside demon beyond our control.

It is hardly surprising that our modern world finds it so difficult to turn away from duality.

In the early dynasties (3050–2600 B.C.), the Pharaoh was seen as the earthly embodiment of Horus, the realized divine principle of the God-King. He was therefore not on the same plane as ordinary mortals; he was a representation of the Cosmic Order. When he died, he would be buried in mud-brick mastabas outside of which would also be buried a wooden boat to carry his spirit to its ultimate destination. Also buried alongside were a number of his servants to serve him in death as in life. In this, and the possible sacrifice of the earlier kings by a priesthood according to laws governed by the stars – the messengers of the Cosmos – there were many similarities with ancient Sumeria.

Then, in the reign of King Zoser (2630–2611 B.C.) of the Third Dynasty, the first known monumental architecture appeared: Zoser's funerary complex at Saqqara, apparently built in stone by a remarkable man whose creative powers seemed to transcend those of normal, mortal beings: Imhotep, at once high priest, doctor, architect, mathematician. From this point on until the end of the Fourth Dynasty in 2465 B.C. there is a flourishing of a civilization which some say has never since been equalled: The Age of the Pyramids – and all of these extraordinary structures came into existence as an expression of the one force which fused the rational and the intuitive into an energy of immeasurable creativity: Mathematics.

In the Egyptian world, mathematics always leads to the Infinite. In mathematics, the rational part of man is in evidence nowadays in the faculty of counting the divided parts; in ancient Egypt, mathematics was essentially an intuitive consciousness of number as an expression of the Infinite Order of the Universe. π and ϕ are universal concepts of number; the number of 3.14 which we attribute to π today is of no relevance as π is a function, a proportion of the Universe. The pyramids themselves were a physical representation of the Universe, (as was all of Egypt's sacred architecture), and they were built on the universal principles of number which we still do not understand in its entirety. These principles were not divisible and are therefore not number as we know it in our day to day world.*

The numbers 1, 2, 3 etc. are, on the other hand, symbols of division. One contains all possibilities of being and non-being and is androgynous. Two is the splitting of 1 and is therefore the manifestation of sexuality, of cerebral intelligence, of the awareness of self through the distinguishing of the 'I' from the 'non I'. Three, being 1 plus 2, is the image of Unity. It can be a return to the Source or continuous expansion in a geometric progression where each phase of growth exceeds the one that goes before it. Each number from 1 to 9 had very specific connotations – what we would view as being somewhat mystical and vague, but which were, for the ancient Egyptians of this era, a pure representation of being.

Nothing that followed ever compared with the pyramids and one can only deduce that the harmony represented by mathematics at its peak – that equal expression of the rational and the intuitive – faded as the Universal significance of number was gradually lost. The degeneration in architecture which followed this great era was a reflection of the degeneration of Egyptian civilization as a whole, a process which continued, with only an occasional exception, until its demise.

The role of the Pharaoh also reflected this degeneration. At the height of the Fourth Dynasty the Triad of the gods of Memphis was one of perfect balance and unity. Ptah was the Cosmic Architect, the giver of form; Sekhmet, his consort, was the equal feminine principle in her dual creative/destructive nature; and Nefertum, the mingling of the male and female creative fire, born anew each morning from the lotus flower. However, above this creative triad, and without whom no creation can take place, is Re, the sun god, the peak of the earlier Heliopolitan Ennead; and, with the beginning of the Fifth Dynasty in 2465 B.C., the Pharaoh is no longer seen as the physical embodiment of Horus, but becomes the son of Re.

This new figure of Re, the sun god, is no longer part of

---

*If you wish to go deeper into this, I suggest you read Schwaller de Lubicz's exhaustive and complex work, *Le Temple de L'Homme*.

the cyclical nature of life returning to Unity with Horus, the tenth god, the human/divine principle. He has now become the solar, male, rational principle presiding over the pharaoh and his people; with his elevation, the rational and the self have begun to hold sway and the connection with the Source begins to fade. It may well have been that a perfect balance between the rational and the intuitive was what ushered in the great era of the Pyramids, but, as the rational gains power and the intuitive crumbles, then the high point of unity and harmony, brief that it was, is left behind.

And so it was that the Fifth and Sixth Dynasties saw the beginning of the decline of art and of the social unity of the hierarchy. The pharaoh was no longer the Pharaoh, the embodiment of divinity, but a mortal at last, a god of second rank, surrounded by a priesthood. Maybe, if one looked at this new type of pharaoh in today's social terms, he would compare favorably as a more compassionate figure – and, indeed, this is where leadership takes on a more human face. Yet, in becoming more human, that sense of oneness with the Infinite is lost. This is neither bad nor good. It is different; it is facing forwards towards the new self-reliant man.

This is also the time of trade, where Egypt loses its insular nature which allowed it to develop unaffected by outside influences and where material preoccupations increasingly encroach upon the spiritual principles of Egyptian life. It sees the rise of the priesthood and a noble merchant class – a broader hierarchy of power, and, with this diffusion of power, the old order almost inevitably crumbles. In the First Intermediate Period of 2150–2040 B.C., the central power of the pharaoh collapses and is replaced by an almost feudal state of warring factions. And yet, in this same period, rec ords show that the 'human' aspect of leadership as we today know it became established. Despite the fact that they fought amongst themselves for power, the leaders of this brief period began to formulate physical laws and tried to dispense justice with as much fairness as they could – as if even they still had the knowledge and understanding that whatever they put out to others in this life would return to them in some way in another life or dimension.

This was the first breakdown of the old order in Egypt, yet the spiritual connection to the Source had not yet so completely disappeared that the result was chaos. Indeed, during this period of change, the old spiritual traditions had been kept alive, so that, when stability returned with the establishment of the Middle Kingdom (2040–1783 B.C.), the power of the pharaoh was restored. On one level, it was as if the original hierarchy had barely changed with the priestly caste as present as ever, yet this new order was on a very different level.

This was the new age of Aries, as seen in the many depictions of the ram in sacred architecture of the time, and a new mentality had developed. In the new capital of Thebes (modern Luxor), there was a new triad of gods: Amon, the animating spirit in living creatures, his consort Mut, and their son Khonsu, who was associated equally with the sun and the moon, with healing and fertility. Amon, although often depicted as Amon-Re (still representing the solar, active principle), was equally seen as Min-Amon, the god of creative sexuality with an erect phallus and carrying a flail.

All is now of a much more physical nature, but still bound closely in consciousness with the spiritual. Even the mysterious invasion by the horse and chariot warriors, the Hyksos, who occupied the land for over 200 years of the Second Intermediate Period, did not break the fundamental tradition of the pharaoh at the head of a structured religious society. The New Kingdom, established following the expulsion of the invaders, ushered in a new era of great architecture and power second only to the Pyramids of the Old Kingdom over seven hundred years earlier.

In particular, the great temples of Luxor and Karnak are awe-inspiring works of majesty. The tradition has still been passed down whereby the Temple is created and constructed as a representation of the Universal principle embodied by the universal numbers π and ϕ, infusing it with a Spirit which transcends the rational and connects the human mind to the Source. Moreover, the Temple of Luxor expresses this unity even further by being built as a representation of the physical body, which, as Schwaller de Lubicz illustrates in his *Temple de l'Homme*, is itself the Temple of the Spirit, within which we mortals play out the sacred cycle of life, expanding our consciousness through experience, confronting the many forms of duality within the physical world of night and day, until we pass through the veil of death into a greater unity enriched by the experience of our lives.

This more human, psychological manifestation of spirituality is much closer to our modern way of thinking than the Universal Authority of the Group, which is a concept beyond our experience. However, once man's personal, physical experience is brought to the forefront of his connection to the Source, the unifying force of group consciousness is displaced by the more expansive and potentially disruptive force of individual consciousness. From this point, it is a matter of free will and choice whether the energy of this individual consciousness is used for the benefit of the Whole or of the Self. In reality, it was only a short step towards man's glorification of himself as the focal center of the Source, of the Universe.

This is exactly what occurs in the period known as the New Kingdom, (1550–1070 B.C.), which also coincides with the Egypt of the Old Testament. The stone sculptures increasingly depict the pharaohs with exaggerated pomp and majesty. The pharaoh himself is surrounded by a class of priests and scribes, which is now hereditary, building a base of power for itself. He is no longer the symbol of God on Earth, Horus, the divine principle; he is now squarely in the fore of the physical world, at the apex of the pyramid of temporal power and material possessions.

Here we come once again, as we did in the last chapter, to that point where the connection to the Whole and between the individual elements of the Whole has become the finest thread, where the power of the individual is ready to be unleashed as the old hierarchy degenerates. During this period, Egypt had ended its isolation and had spread out into Mesopotamia in order to protect its frontiers, but this contact itself no doubt diluted the singular energy of its civilization. The New Kingdom was the final flurry of magnificence and opulence before the decline set in. This time, when the armed Iron Age hordes swept into the land, there was no return to its former glory.

And yet, this was by no means the end of Egyptian culture, but rather ushered in a new era when Egyptian influence was swept far beyond the confines of its boundaries by the same powers which had annexed Egypt as part of their own expanding empires. With the invasion by the Persian king Cambyses, father of Darius I, in 525 B.C., Egyptian beliefs and culture began to infuse into the two most powerful civilizations of the time: Persia itself and, of even more significance, Greece, with whom Egypt had allied herself to try to expel the Persian invader.

Although it was less than two hundred years later that Alexander the Great himself conquered Egypt, this intervening period in Greece provided the most fertile climate of intellectual inquiry our world has ever known. How much of this was due to the influence of Egyptian civilization we may never fully know, for the highest elements of Egyptian knowledge and learning were kept hidden within the secret Mystery Schools, once it became apparent that the physical land of Egypt would remain under foreign control.

What we do know, though, is that, even when occupied by the brutal Persians, the welcomed Alexander or the materially exploiting Romans, the external form of Egyptian religion was allowed to continue unabated – in particular under the rule of the Ptolemies, the inheritors of the Alexandrian legacy, when monumental architecture flourished once again.

Ultimately, though, it was confronted by one rigid force against which it was powerless: Christianity. Even under early imperial Rome after the defeat of Cleopatra, the traditional Egyptian spiritual practice was at least initially tolerated, (just as the Egyptians themselves had tolerated Christianity as one of many 'mystery' religions of the time); yet, its death knell came when the Roman Emperor Constantine put all of his imperial power behind Christianity, adopting it as the state religion and, at the Council of Nicaea, imposed a rigid, intolerant creed which denounced all other religions as heretical.

This marked the end of the incomparable Egyptian civilization, as far as we recognize it. The last temple to fall to the Christian zealots in 495 A.D. was Philae, left abandoned in the middle of the upper reaches of the Nile – the huge reliefs facing the setting sun of the West completely obliterated, those facing the East left untouched, maybe awaiting the dawn, when the ancient, inner mysteries will be revealed to us once more!

Chapter 5

Greece and the Secularization of Thought

If the disintegration of Egypt could be considered as the end of the old order, the sudden flowering of the Greek city-states is certainly the beginning of the new. In the few hundred years in which this amazing civilization was at its peak, the hallmarks of our modern world were imprinted within the consciousness of Western man – at first within the small area of its birth, but, after its decline, spread throughout the Western world and beyond by the three great empires of Alexander, Rome and Christendom.

As with each pivotal era of man's development, there seems to be no gradual, discernible movement towards the momentous change in consciousness. Once more, we see an apparent blossoming of the new out of the decline of the old: the individual, rational mind, in the guise of inquiring, philosophical thought, emerges from the ashes of the old, more unified order and creates a view of the world and man's place in it which has fundamentally survived until today, two thousand years later.

The earliest known 'civilization' in the geographical area of Greece was the Minoan culture on the island of Crete, south of the Greek mainland. Along with Mesopotamia, Egypt and Harappa, this was one of the great centers of immense cultural richness whose influence gradually expanded far beyond its borders from the middle of the third millennium B.C. onwards. Archaeological research points to an essentially agricultural, non-heroic society with the image of the female goddess abounding in the works of art of this era.

The Greek mainland, on the other hand, was subject to a completely different set of influences, as streams of nomadic hordes poured their way down from the north. The Aryans followed their herds southwards from the southern Russian plains, conquering, settling, and most important, absorbing the existing communities in their path. These essentially male-dominated tribes worshipped their own Nature Gods, but were tolerant of other gods, often recognizing their own deities in alien cults, such as Athena, the goddess of war. As their simple, nomadic life had needed no cohesive outer structure, they assimilated much from the communities they overran and, ultimately, were themselves seduced not only by the relative ease of an agricultural, settled existence, but also by what came to be an obsession with the pride of individual possession.

After the fall of the Minoan civilization in Crete around 1500 B.C., it is the male, heroic, active principle which reigns supreme in Greek culture. Although many of the existing female goddesses were drawn into the new hierarchy of gods, they were, like Athena, given masculine roles, or were symbolic of certain female characteristics which were considered subsidiary to the more 'powerful' male attributes. The female mysteries of the mother/serpent/moon with their eternal cycles, which regained their original power in the East after a short period of Aryan control, were, in Greece, driven into the subconscious realms by the dazzling light of this forward driving male energy. In Greek mythology, there are numerous examples of the power of the female being tapped by or, more often, being subdued by the male, heroic spirit: the archetypal hero, Perseus, cuts off the head of the bewitching Medusa; in Delphi, at the temple of Apollo the god of light and reason, the male, phallic, stone shaft of the Omphalos is driven through the head of the serpent goddess in order to tap the mysterious energies of the Earth; Athena herself is born from the brain of Zeus, the king of the gods.

One could say that at least there was intermarriage between

the gods and goddesses, unlike in the Levant, where the assumption of one supreme male god denied even the existence of the creative female principle. However, compared with ancient Egypt, where the gods were representations of the various attributes of creation and of mankind, these Greek gods were one further step from unity with the Source. The Universal principles symbolized within each member of the Egyptian, divine hierarchy had now become mere human attributes, with each Greek god exhibiting the personality traits and aggressive tendencies of the people who created him. Individual human power and the free will which came with it were now the focus of this new material world.

Modern Greece could be said to begin with the civilization of Mycaenae – in a sense, the cross-point of two distinct cultures. The Mycaeneans were distinctly Northern and originally nomadic, but, in settling at the time that the Minoan civilization began to expand its boundaries, they were introduced to all the high arts of civilization mentioned in previous chapters. When the great city of Knossos and the Minoan civilization collapsed, the already expanding power of Mycaenae was there to fill the vacuum and assume control of this geographical area of the Mediterranean.

The only real knowledge we have of these fabled people is through the epics of Homer, which were written long after the Mycaenaean civilization itself collapsed and was overrun by other invading hordes from the North: the Dorians. The image we have, whether it is a true one or a projection of its own characteristics by later culture, is of a Heroic Age, symbolized on the one hand by the supposedly historical siege of Troy, where honor is of the essence in this conflict between two great powers, and on the other hand by the mysterious, mythical journey of the Odyssèy.

These two aspects of this era, as depicted by Homer, were to have an immense impact on later Greek civilization in the way that they were integrated into all aspects of Greek life and thought. In the battle for Troy, the 'arete' of Achilles and other heroes – best interpreted as the expression of personal excellence and esteem – was the male purity which all Greeks, whether philosophers or statesmen, strove for. It came to represent not only individual physical prowess, courage and honor, but also the shining light of the rational mind's urge to know and discover the truth. It is the very essence of the Western ideal: the knight in shining white armor, striding forwards courageously, allowing nothing to block the path of his individual quest.

Odysseus is the personification of this ideal, yet his quest in Homer's *Odyssey* involves something much deeper, less concrete. There is almost a shamanic quality about his long and arduous journey during which he is repeatedly faced with the most rigorous, yet also symbolic tests. Many of the obstacles he faces represent the deep, subconscious energies which lie hidden beneath the courageous exterior of the archetypal male hero: as he crosses the veil of mortal life to and back from the Underworld, he must face an existence beyond the shining light of his own heroic world; as he meets the mythic female figures of Circe and Calypso among others, he is faced with his own suppressed, female nature which he must integrate within himself before finally returning to his hearth and home kept alight by his wife. The whole story – in essence an individual's search for Unity in a world beset by conflict and duality – is pervaded with a sense of mysticism which was evidently inherent in early Greek life, but which was gradually lost as the great philosophers turned their minds more and more to the material world.

The tumult of the collapse of the Mycaenaean empire was simultaneous with the wars in Mesopotamia and the degeneration in Egypt which seemed to mark this era. As the Dorians swept down from the North, all the hallmarks of this culture, including writing, were lost, as mainland Greece as we now know it underwent a temporary Dark Age.

This is where the scene now shifts to the Western coast of what is now Turkey and to the site of the real emergence of the Greek mind. Just before 1000 B.C., first the Aeolians, and then the Ionians, fleeing from the Dorian invasion, came to settle in this part of what was called Anatolia. We know little about the existing inhabitants, except that their prime object of worship was the female goddess connected to the Earth. Whether they were refugees from the ancient Minoan civilization or whether they were solely people who had migrated from the East, nobody knows for sure. What we do know, though, is that the combination of the original inhabitants, the Ionian settlers and maybe some other force of which we know nothing was responsible for the rise of a truly remarkable culture in the individual city-states which suddenly sprang up on these rocky outcrops overlooking the Mediterranean.

The Ionian confederacy grew at an astonishing rate and shortly came to consist of twelve sophisticated, self-reliant city-states, of which Miletus was the largest and most powerful. It was here, not in Athens, where the inquiring mind of the Greeks first formulated the Question which has been accredited as the origin of philosophical thought as we know it: 'What is the Earth made of?' – in other words, a rational attempt to understand the Universe in material terms.

Now, this may not seem to us to be an earth-shattering question, yet the very act of asking the Question set the human mind rolling irrevocably along the path of philosophical inquiry which has fundamentally created the society we live in today. It is the point at which the Western active principle breaks away from the relative disengagement inherent in both Egyptian and Eastern thought – where there is now an expansive search for complexity as opposed to the Eastern and Egyptian yearning to return to the Source, and where the outer world of form rules over the inner nature of man.

Yet, despite this split, the mystical elements of Eastern religion were not cast off overnight, as we have seen from the Odyssey, whose author Homer lived in the Ionian confederacy. However, the emphasis at this time was on the Orphic religion – one of denial and discipline, whereby the body is perceived as holding the soul in bondage and the soul can only be released into unity with the Source through asceticism. This profoundly influenced the first pre-Socratic philosophers, as they are termed, although for them, this asceticism did not lead towards a Unity with the Source. Instead, it served to liberate the rational mind, which, when undisturbed by the sensations of pleasure and pain, could enter into the pure discipline of active inquiry in order to create laws and understanding from the realms of human judgment alone.

Of course, the question arises: Why is it that systematic, rational inquiry should have its origin in Ionia?

In many ways, this Eastern part of the Mediterranean was a fertile crossover point between the older, more spiritually based cultures of the East and the new, free-wheeling culture spreading from the North, the individualistic nature of which had been well adapted to the sparse, rocky coastline of the Ionian settlements.

The two greatest influences from the East at this time came from the powerful Persian Empire of Darius Ist, which was ultimately to be the downfall of the Ionian confederacy, and from Egypt, with whom the Ionians had entered into a brief alliance against the mutual threat of the Persians. At its peak, the Persian Empire enveloped the whole area of Mesopotamia that was considered to be the cradle of civilization, and therefore could not help but absorb the knowledge and culture which had originated there. In addition, Darius Ist was a fervent disciple of Zoroaster.

Zoroaster is a fascinating, if somewhat nebulous,* undocumented figure. Being antecedent to both Buddha and Christ, he could be called the first great prophet to preach the concept of a monotheistic Divinity. As opposed to the concept of the Fall of Man from Unity into Duality, he spread the idea of Duality as an original state: of the God of Light, Ahura Mazda, in perpetual conflict with Angra Mainyu, the Deceiver, the principle of the lie.

What is very Greek about Zoroaster's teachings is his opposition to the more passive Eastern view of cyclical destruction and regeneration. He advocated an optimistic faith in the ultimate victory for the Light, gained through the responsibility of each individual choosing to engage in the fight for good over evil. This was the first 'ethical' religion whose major precept was that the world could be changed by human action. It was also, not coincidentally, the first materialistic religion in which it was better to be strong than weak, rich than poor, to have a house and family than no house and family.

This materialistic ethic was very much in existence in Miletus at the peak of Ionian civilization in the sixth century B.C., although the individualistic nature of the Ionian cities could not have been in stronger contrast to the centrally controlled Persian Empire which spread Zoroaster's teachings. Thales of Miletus, the man accredited with being the first man to ask

---

*If he was indeed an individual man, his dates have been put at anywhere after 1200 B.C.

The Question 'What is the Earth made of?', was an expert astronomer/astrologer, who used his knowledge to foresee a bumper olive harvest and therefore went out and cornered the olive press market, so that he could sell them off at a great profit! He also thanked God for three things: for being a human and not an animal, a man and not a woman, a Greek and not a barbarian – a typically Greek arrogant and isolationist view, which contributed much to the rise and ultimately to the fall of Greek civilization.

Indeed, along this rocky coastline, we see a civilization which differs from any which had preceded it – in particular in the way that the power of the individual has successfully taken hold and still managed to maintain order through some kind of collective responsibility. There is no central authority of religion or of kingship; despite the existence of a new structure of inequality of citizen over slave, of man over woman, the flourishing of these new, independent Ionian states represents the dawning of a new society of reason and of continuous exploration where man takes his destiny into his own hands.

The answer that Thales made to The Question* was that the fundamental element of the Earth was Water; this was succeeded by Anaximanes' premise that Air came prior to Water, and then by Heraclitus that Fire preceded Air. The essence behind all these first 'natural philosophers' is that they saw aspects of matter as the principle behind all creation, demonstrating the immense leap that this new culture had made away from the spiritual traditions of all high civilizations which had preceded them.

This dualism of matter and spirit is pivotal in the evolution of human thought and behavior, for, however much subsequent philosophers may have tried to reconcile the spiritual and physical worlds, these attempts have always been bound by the rational mind which was responsible for the separation in the first place.

Bound within this material view of the world, the pre-Socratics vied with each other to create a world view that

---

*Supposedly in 585 B.C.

was acceptable to a mentality which saw the earth and man firmly set in the center of the Universe. Inherent in this discussion was the essence of dualism, the need to reconcile those opposing tendencies which created change and conflict in the world. One pupil of Thales, Anaximander, proposed that all opposites returned to the 'Boundless' as an atonement for causing strife. In answer to his question of 'What keeps the earth in its place', he concluded that the earth was symmetrically in the center of the Universe and therefore needed no outside support.

Heraclitus, on the other hand, saw strife itself as the motivating principle which kept the world alive, so that duality was a creative force of energy, only able to be reconciled by the wisdom of man; while Empedocles added a more cyclical, even mystical view, whereby strife was responsible for separating the four elements of Fire, Air, Water and Earth, raising each in turn over the other three. For him, the one thing which would bind them together was Love; also, starting from these same principles, he saw Health as the balance between all these opposite forces, prefiguring the medical theories of Hippocrates.

In focusing on strife in this way, both Heraclitus and Empedocles acknowledged the creative/destructive force of duality which many later philosophers failed to do. This may have much to do with the emphasis of these early thinkers on the four elements, which for them signified not only the physical essence of Earth, Water, Air and Fire but also the active principles which they represented within the psyche of man. These essential energies within each human being are to this day still recognized in the East, but have been dismissed as irrelevant superstition by the Western rational mentality. Only in a few esoteric teachings such as the Kabbalah has an understanding of the power of the Elements been retained in the West.

The one great philosopher from this region and of this era who felt a close connection to the old Unity was Pythagoras, whom we of course view as more of a mathematician. In fact, his mathematical theories were inextricably linked with his mysticism and this is where the powerful influence of Egyptian thought comes into play.

The secret teachings from the Egyptian Mystery Schools were at the heart of Pythagoras' philosophy. Bound within his belief in reincarnation and purification of the soul was a belief that philosophical inquiry was the only way of transcending physical reality so that the soul could climb upwards to the next level. His philosophical quest was for the first cause and principle of all things, and, drawing on that very Egyptian earthly representation of the Universe, he perceived this first cause as being Number, not only evident in the building of the great Egyptian edifices, but also audible in the heavenly spheres of Music.

Music was evidently a very important part of early Greek life. Despite the Ionian and Greek ascetic interpretation of the Orphic religion, Orpheus was of course the son of Apollo, and both were very much associated not only with musical creativity but also with healing, which reflected the understanding at this time that the harmony and balance within music could also harmonize the elemental forces within the physical body.

Pythagoras's relation to music was both mystical and rational. He saw the harmony of music reflecting the harmony of the Universe, but he is of course best known for investigating its physical proportions in relation to number. Later generations have concentrated on this theoretical, mathematical side of his work, and have tended to dismiss the importance of the mystical element of his teachings.

In reality, although he saw the contrary nature of duality as the motivating principle of all things, he saw unity, represented by number in its universal sense, above this as the substance of all things. He vehemently believed in the harmony and natural order of the world, governed by a cohesive force which lay behind and within all creation. His rational probings were an expression of his spiritual connection to the Whole, fulfilling a need to present a view of the physical world which was intelligible to man.

At the same time, however, he was still profoundly influenced by the Orphic religion which saw the rational, immaterial soul as being distinct from and superior to the body and the defective world of the senses. This elevation of mind/spirit on the one hand over body/senses on the other was the first step towards the creation of a fundamental imbalance within the trinity of body, mind and spirit – a process which would culminate in a form of duality which would have been completely alien to him and which would have struck at the heart of his own core principles: the separation of rational thought from spiritual understanding.

It is important to remember that the humanistic/religious notion of Greek gods was still pervasive in Greek society, in particular in Athens, where another Miletian philosopher, Anaxagoras, was prosecuted for the impious view that there was one intelligent substance which lay behind the world, rather than the gods on Mount Olympus. His notion of this ordered, natural substance, the 'nous', immanent in all living things, brings God down to the level of some physical form – a premise which not only negates the power of the Olympian gods, but which also raises the immutable physical form above the expansive nature of Pythagorean intelligence.

This rocky path was followed even further by Parmenides and his Eleatic school of followers in the first half of the fifth century B.C. (Elea was a province in Southern Italy under Ionian influence.) Parmenides, an ex-disciple of Pythagoras who wrote in verse, had far-reaching influence with his concept of eternal, unchanging, uncreated being. Everything, in his eyes, pertained to material reality. What could not be thought of therefore could not be, as one cannot think of nothing. The material world quite simply is, but empty space is not, therefore does not exist. As an extension of this, his disciple Zeno denied the existence of infinite space, for if the earth was contained in space, what would contain it in turn?

This logic may seem very odd and childlike to us, and this indeed could be termed the infancy of philosophical thought. Yet, its influence and the mentality behind it were very real, leading both to the denial of an infinite Source of Being and to the beginning of a materialistic, empirical world view, in which the Source needed to be defined in human, rationally comprehensible terms. The subsequent 'atomist' theory of Leucippus that atoms moved in empty space in order to give solidity to emptiness finally denied room for any reality outside the physical – a belief largely embraced by science right up to the twentieth century, during which the unpredictable and infinite divisibility of quantum mechanics has opened even scientists' minds to the possibility of a deeper reality beyond the scope of our rational minds.

These early forays into rational inquiry, despite their seeming naiveté to us now, should not be underestimated in their influence on the 'great philosophers' of the Athenian Golden Age who in their turn laid many of the foundations for our modern world view.

The high point of this Golden Age only lasted the sixty years from the great victory at Marathon in 490 B.C., when the Athenians defeated the same Persian army which had only just overcome the Ionian confederacy, to the beginning of the Peloponnesian War. At its peak, the city of Athens became the center of the most diverse cultural, social and creative activity that the Western world has probably ever seen – indeed, at this point in history, it was as if the whole of the old world was being transformed into something completely new, for this was also the era of Buddha in India and of Confucius in China, each of whose influence, like the Greek civilization, was spread by others after their death far beyond the narrow confines of their immediate, geographical area. The cultures of the East and West were, in this era, set on their own very different courses.

In this new great city of Athens, whose population reached at its peak a quarter of a million people, everything was brought to a human, physical level. A new social order was created; artistic expression expanded into new forms; a new breed of thinking encompassing all aspects of the physical life was born. The creative potential of man had been truly unleashed.

Inherent within this expansion of culture was the acceptance of individual responsibility and free will:

An Athenian citizen does not neglect the state because he takes care of his own household; and even those of us who are engaged in business have a fair idea of politics. We alone regard a man who takes no interest in public affairs, not as harmless, but as a useless character; and if a few of us are originators, we are all sound judges of a policy. The great impediment to action is, in our opinion, not discussion, but the want of that knowledge which is gained by discussion preparatory to action. For we have a peculiar power of thinking before we act and of acting too, whereas other men are courageous from ignorance but hesitate upon reflection. And they are surely esteemed the bravest spirits who, having the clearest sense both of the pains and pleasures of life, do not on that account shrink from danger.

These famous words by Pericles, the foremost figure of state during this Golden Age, and, as it happens, a former pupil of Anaxagoras, sum up the essence of the role of the individual within the ideal Greek 'polis'.* The emphasis on participation, discussion and knowledge lays the framework for democracy in its purest form, which has little in common with the non-participatory democracy of our modern world. The power is invested in the community, whereby the rule of law is for the common good, but where also any citizen has the right to vote or speak in any legislative or judicial body. This is no rigid structure in which the power of the people to vote for a representative every four years or so gives an illusory sense of freedom; this is a society built upon the responsibility of each individual to participate and create his own reality. As summed up in that final sentence above from Pericles, this world is a celebration of the totality of human experience and the lessons to be learned from it.

Of course, also inherent within this speech of Pericles is the Greek scorn for 'other men', which brings us back to Thales' superiority of Greek over barbarian, man over woman as well as citizen over non-citzen. However, this unequal structure within Athenian society, with the new governing élite of the 'citizens' forming a minority in number yet holding absolute power, must still be seen in the perspective of its time: there existed within the 'polis' a greater sharing of power than in any hierarchical civilization which had preceded it and the majority of those which followed it.

This arrogance no doubt contributed to the fall of this great 'experiment', but its main weakness lay in the fact

---

*Although it is usually translated as 'Greek city-state', the word 'polis' originally had a much deeper connotation of 'community'.

that the group consciousness could not ultimately contain the diverse powers of the individual which it promoted so fervently — especially in a society more and more immersed in materialism. The laws of the 'polis' very much focused on the material concerns of its citizens such as the right to own property, enter into legal marriage etc., and, as has been repeated again and again in the history of mankind, such a strong material ethic combined with inequality leads always to instability and conflict, weakening the fabric of society and exposing it to the threat of a more powerful outside force.

Any innate, spiritual binding force within the group was minimal. Government was totally secular, although paying lip-service to the 'gods'. Temples were builtm ore as a glorification of man's power than as an expression of man's connection to the Source; oracles were consulted and sacrifices were performed, but these were always in relation to specific activities pertaining to the day-to-day life of the city. Universal principles had now left the sphere of religion and passed into the realm of philosophy.

Even art had been affected by the mind/body dualism, in that the separation of mind from body had unleashed the physical aspect of man as a separate entity unto itself to be worshipped for all its inherent glory, in its aspect of the male, human form. Art itself had become a representation of the sacredness of physical beauty with gods and heroes alike depicted as ideal human types. Leaving behind the old forms of Egyptian sculptures attached to a rigid backdrop, the new, individual, Greek style of a free-standing, three dimensional, alive figure was a celebration of man in the center of the Universe: the youthful, naked, heroic, male figure contrasting with the female figure, which, in Greek art, was generally portrayed clothed and serene.

This coincided with the rise of purely physical 'love', represented by Eros, son of Aphrodite. As the ancient connection to the Whole had faded, the new connection was made through the worship of Beauty — the physical beauty of an individual as a mirror of the Beauty or Perfection inherent in the Universe itself.

And then there were the philosophers — neither practicing their art in the limited way we view philosophy today, nor being confined to their predecessors' search for a primal, 'natural'

Cause. The three giants of Greek philosophical thought — Socrates, Plato and Aristotle — would accept no limitation as to the scope of their inquiry. Bound within the culture of their upbringing and yet also breaking out beyond these boundaries, celebrating the free will and spirit of man yet always searching for a way back to the Source, these three men left no stone unturned, no old belief or tradition unchallenged; but their final legacy was one of so many unanswered questions that they left in their wake a world of infinite uncertainty and possibilities. The old order was a relic of the past; the search for a new order had barely begun.

The era of the three great philosophers in Athens was at a time when the decay and corruption of the ideal of the 'polis' were well underway with the ideal of democracy being perverted by those who began to abuse power for their own personal ends. Their writings must therefore be seen very much in the light of looking back to a lost ideal and trying to recreate a new, definable order which could be applied practically according to universal principles.

Nothing written by Socrates has ever been found and probably never existed, for his philosophy was inseparable from oral communication and active participation within the community as opposed to his successors' drier, more logical presentation through the written word. We owe what we know about Socrates to his greatest pupil, Plato, who recorded in his own style many of the discourses in which Socrates participated with his pupils and his many rivals.

Socrates was an individual who stood in opposition to what he saw as a climate of degeneration in his beloved Athens — and in particular to the Sophists, an expedient yet powerful band of 'educators' who trained their pupils in, among other things, rhetoric — a dubious art which was more concerned with winning an argument or persuading a court than searching for the truth.

Truth, or Good, was the essential starting point of the philosophical inquiry of Socrates. He had no interest in the physical science of the pre-Socratics; his science was clarity, honesty and truth, clearing away false definitions and ideas in order to delve into the essence of a matter in debate. In keeping with his own free-wheeling lifestyle, his focus was on the individual life or argument rather than the unified system of morality which his followers tried to attain and which he would no doubt have considered pompous.

He had turned his back on materialism, having no concern with worldly possessions, so that, in having no ties, he could pursue a purely disinterested means of inquiry. The aim of his dialectic was to reach the supreme starting point: the pure form of Good. He was the essential humanist, seeing God as human Good, which could only be attained through knowledge in its two aspects: that which can be learned and that which is innate within oneself.

The aim of education was to learn to think for oneself, touching the well of inner knowledge – a principle which harks back to Pythagoras' transmigration of the soul. In his eyes, man erred only through lack of knowledge (in stark contrast to the later Christian ethic where too much knowledge was viewed as a path to sin!). Knowledge was attained through the clarity of reason.

One cannot be sure that this was not an idealized portrait of a man by his devoted pupil, but the image we have of Socrates as a human being is one who is equally at peace with the inner and outer world and who harmonizes his rational, dialectic method of inquiry with the intuitive connection he has to his personal notion of God. He is the personification of the Athenian enlightened being, and was therefore a threat to the degenerate establishment which was at that time presiding over the demise of this once 'ideal' society.

Socrates the man, however, compares favorably with his theoretical, philosophical legacy. Where he acted in the world at large as a living example of his beliefs, he stood out like a shining light. When he tried to define his principles in a universal sense, his theories became full of paradoxes.

As an extension of his belief that man erred only through lack of knowledge, he deduced that no man therefore willingly erred. Also, he insisted on his theory of the unity of virtues, in that either one had all the virtues such as courage, honor and justice, which were reflections of one's inner soul, or one had none at all!

In both of these assumptions, he adhered strictly to his ideal of the Good, rather than accepting the existence of human frailty and emotion, which was in evidence not only in the people all around him, but as depicted in all its unadulterated detail in the theatre and literature of his day.

This was the essential paradox of Socrates, and one which came back to haunt his successors. In an ideal world full of people such as Socrates, his theories would be just and applicable; in a world which has strayed far from the ideal and which is governed by self-interest, his more universal theories were almost an irrelevance. What made him such a great man and teacher was the living example he gave to those around him; his theories were of such a beautiful simplicity that they could not encompass the growing complexity of a society in which the emotions and desires of ordinary men were turning further away from the search for Good or God.

In bringing God down to the human level of Good, he had irrevocably changed the direction of human thought and inquiry. When man searches for God as the Source of All Being, his quest is the return to Unity; in searching for Good on the physical plane, man sets out on the expansive path of human experience, so that he may, through his own actions and the activity of his mind, feel his own individual sense of the divine rightness of being.

This is of course the essence of the human condition, but what Socrates failed to take into account was that the world was not full of Socrates; nor was it even governed by men such as Socrates. In the essentially material world that existed even in his day, only a handful of men would follow this conscious path towards the Good; the majority would be enmeshed in their own material and emotional lives, yielding their broader responsibilities to others.

This dilemma of the ideal and 'real' worlds was to obsess those who tried to define the notion of Good after the death of Socrates; and, of course, the more they tried to define Good in material, external terms, the further it led them from God, the indefinable Source of All Being. The constantly expanding and changing world of duality can never be defined in rigid terms, and any attempt to impose an immutable structure upon it is always doomed to ultimate failure. The only space which can contain this duality is the infinity of Unity whence it came.

It seems therefore almost fitting that Socrates should end his days condemned to death by a society which felt more and more threatened by the individual conscience and power which he represented, and, in taking his own life, he asserted that power even in death. He was a remarkable man who had outlived his own time but whose influence was to far outlive him. His death in 399 B.C. marked the end of an era. His greatest influence came not so much from the individual elements of his philosophy, but rather from the fact that he took his philosophical inquiry away from the infinity of 'God' towards the finite world of human Good. As a man, Socrates had represented the pinnacle of the Athenian ideal of the self-reliant man searching for the Good. Once this creative aspect of the individual seeker of Truth had been condemned and destroyed, the divisive nature of the individual separated from his connnection to the Whole was free to assert itself in ways which were not necessarily for the Common Good.

The powerful need to define Good lay at the heart of the huge body of work written by Plato and Aristotle, the heirs of Socrates whose influence in shaping our modern world far exceeds any other philosophers who have followed them.

Plato was born in 428 B.C., the year after the death of Pericles. This was at a time when Athens was already in decline, a very important fact when considering the essence of both his and Aristotle's philosophical thought. Theirs was not a heralding in or celebration of a Golden Age; it was rather a looking back at a recent Golden Age, searching for the reasons for its decline; and ultimately an attempt, through the power of reason, to recreate a 'perfect' society within an institutional framework which would harness the 'good' of its citizens.

Whereas Socrates always spoke to and focused on the individual, Plato extended his scope to the polis. Confronted by a decaying society, Plato felt a need to create order and to fight the scepticism which was increasingly taking hold of his fellow citizens. Sadly, as we shall see, his ultimate legacy was to do exactly the opposite, despite or maybe even due to the fact that he combined an honest quest for the Good with the most brilliant rational mind of his day.

What concerned him most was the metaphysical essence of things and the structure of an ideal society, the former having a great bearing on the latter. His approach was very much in between the free-wheeling inquiry of Socrates and the later 'cold logic' of Aristotle, and, in certain ways, Plato can be seen as a powerful transition figure who tried to bring together the Pandora's Box of his predecessors' ideas into a unified order which could be comprehended and built on (and misinterpreted) by future generations.

Plato was pulled in opposing directions by the legacy of two of the pre-Socratics already mentioned, Heraclitus and Parmenides, and much of his energy was spent trying to reconcile them. On the one hand, there was the dynamic eternal flux of Heraclitus caused by the prime motivating force of strife between opposing principles; on the other hand, there was the static immutable reality of Parmenides' material, indestructible world.

At the root of this opposition was the more fundamental conflict within himself between the mystical and the rational. In his writings, one sees the constant struggle between his mystical nature which searches for the Truth without any bounds and his rational side which searches for Universals which can be defined. With his theory of Forms, it is as if he is searching for an explainable Order which will reflect the supreme Idea of Good/God, and he does so by trying to delve into the essence of things and impose a correlation between the changing world of what the senses perceive and the immutable world of universal ideas and precepts. He accepted the Pythagorean belief that the physical world is intelligible in terms of number, but extended this concept to create his own, new world of Forms in which the immaterial, unchanging essence which lay behind all things could only be perceived through purely intellectual thought. This was the ultimate reality, while the world of sense perceptions was the fleeting world of illusion.

However mystical Plato's personal beliefs may have been, his formulation of this Theory of Forms creates a new level of being which separated the physical world even further from the Source. In the East, the world of the senses is also seen as 'maya', the world of illusion, but the world of reality is the eternal world of the Spirit in which all is connected to the Source. In Egypt and in the mind of Pythagoras, number was an expression of the harmony of the Universe, quite different from Plato's perspective of the world of Forms, which placed the rational quite firmly over the material world with little acknowledgment of any force beyond the rational, such as Spirit.

Here we have the essential division of body, mind and spirit, and it formalizes a dualistic way of thinking which profoundly influenced those who came after Plato, not least of all the Christian Church.

What is more, Plato's attempt to create a concept of objective reality with all imperfections removed destroys the validity of a subjective, individual reality and the fluidity which is required to adapt to a constantly changing world. This was, of course, not Plato's intention, as his ideal was for the supremacy of the inquiring mind searching for the Good. However, by formulating rigid ideas to try and create a sense of order in the physical world, he left the door open for those who wished to impose their own 'moral' order upon others – in particular, in this new world of the separation of body, mind and spirit, those who wished to use a 'higher authority' to suppress all that pertained to the body and the senses.

Obviously, there is much more to Plato's philosophical theory than what I have just outlined, and the originality of his thoughts was remarkable in his era. There is little doubt that he was deeply committed to the ideal of the Good or Truth, yet the more he tried to create an artificial, comprehensible order out of the limitlessness of the Universe, the more he created a separate world of ideas which was cut off from any innate connection with that same Universal Whole.

His attempt to bring his ideal of Good in line with politics had very much the same effect. The dilemma of all political theorists is to create a framework in which the good of the many can be achieved, notwithstanding the self-interest of man, and Plato, observing the decline of the Athenian ideal of the freedom and participation of its citizens, was painfully aware of this dilemma.

He was confronted by the same problem as Socrates: that not all men were such as he, who constantly sought after the Truth and the Good. This is what finally made him abandon his initial ideal of an absolute philosopher-king, for he realized that no one man could be trusted not to abuse absolute power.

What is interesting about his idea of a philosopher-king in the first place is that it harks back in many ways to the ideal of the Pharaoh. The ideal of the Pharaoh or the God-King is of a being who is connected to the Source of All Being and who therefore, by nature, will act for the Good of his people. With Plato's philosopher-king, this 'connection' is interpreted in terms of individual conscience and a sense of responsibility, but the ideal is still the same.

We of course know how the ideal of the Pharaoh degenerated and Plato was no doubt swayed by observing the corruption of the society around him. His ideal of the philosopher-king had arisen in opposition to the decaying ruins of the 'democratic' ideal which he saw around him, but, in the end, he abandoned this and succumbed to the need to formulate a structure the prime goal of which was stability and order.

As opposed to the idealistic nature of the philosopher-king, Plato's new political divisions were very much more on a pragmatic, material level. He proposed three classes: Guardians, whose main attribute was wisdom; Soldiers, whose main attribute was courage; and Laborers, whose main attribute was hoped to be moderation. The reason of the Guardians would prevail over the temper of the Soldiers which would contain the appetite of the Laborers. This hierarchy of course depends on the altruism of the ruling class of Guardians, and, because of the potential for abuse, Plato suggested that they should own no personal possessions and have their children taken away at birth.

When we consider that this was the first written down, formulated, political theory, born from an essentially pessimistic outlook, it is amazing how this fundamental structure of inequality came to be institutionalized in various forms within Western civilization until the modern version of democracy came along. But, on the other hand, it is hardly surprising, because, by sanctioning this unequal structure where the power is in the hands of the few, Plato once again plays unwittingly into the hands of those whose primary ambition is to gain the advantages of power for themselves. He further consolidates this by raising the code of law over all things, defining Law as the reflection of a perfect Universe governed by reason, thereby giving free rein to those who would justify as being 'God's will' any law they choose to impose.

The one final aspect of Plato's teaching which has profoundly affected our modern world view is his attitude towards education. When Greek civilization was at its peak, education was not a particularly formal business. It was more intuitive and physical than intellectual: music, art and the oral tradition of Homer's epics came before the written word. Later on, education in rhetoric and practical matters was taken on by the Sophists so despised by Socrates, but it was not until Plato that a formal theory of education was written down.

Needless to say, the rational reigned supreme in Plato's ideal, with all else considered superfluous. The mythical elements of Greek tradition were considered to be unreliable and even disruptive, because, as Plato so literally said, 'the gods behaved badly.'! This narrow rational view has gone beyond the point where any universal truths can be gleaned from myth; truth can only be attained through the rational mind.

Likewise, music was dismissed by him as something for children to occupy themselves for their imagination. Gone is the understanding of music at the core of Pythagoras' philosophical thought as an expression of divine harmony, not only through the effect of its sound, but through the more rational science of mathematics.

For Plato, the aim of education was to direct the trained mind away from the temporal, physical world towards the absolute, eternal world of essence and forms. We see here the ascetic influence of the early Orphic Greeks, where the tumult of the world, including the richness of our emotional lives, must be shut out in order for one to attain the Truth – hence Plato's concern about the Tragic theatre of his day, which he saw as unnecessarily arousing potentially destructive emotions within men.

In this world of cold clarity, he takes as his starting point Mathematics, deprived of the mystical nuances of Pythagoras, and leads on to the final discipline of Dialectics – the essence of the rational training to define things through logical argument. This exclusive emphasis on the rational, with any expression of intuitive creativity perceived as a subsidiary activity, is our educational heritage which survives unquestioned to this very day. It is at the root of our immense achievements on the physical plane; it is also at the root of our uncaring society.

As you have no doubt gathered, I see the influence of this one man as being pivotal in the evolution of our species into the modern man as we see ourselves today. Everything he wrote down he did in the most honest spirit, and yet the aspects of his teachings which had the most influence on the society we live in today were those which could most readily be misinterpreted and abused.

But, then, this is what the world of duality is all about: free will and choice. When the individual no longer has an innate sense of the natural harmony of Unity and of the infinite connection of all living beings, then he is thrown into a new, vast world of individual responsibility, where man as a race is ultimately responsible for his own destiny.

Plato was the first man to try and write down a system which would help mankind to follow the path towards Truth and Good. What comprised this system were his personal reflections on God, attained through reason. Where he erred was to scorn the emotional nature of man, for, in doing so, he ignored an elemental force within the human race which was not subject to reason and which would lead us far away from his ideal of the Good.

If Plato was the speculative philosopher for whom reason was the means of reaching Good/God and of creating a world which reflected this divine perfection, then Aristotle was the analytical philosopher more concerned with the down-to-earth matters of men. While Plato's emphasis on the rational drew the human mind further from the Source and into the world of duality, the philosophy of Aristotle completed this process by firmly embedding the human mind in the material world.

In later years, Plato and Aristotle were seen in opposition to one another. Plato was the mystical humanist who turned his eyes to Heaven – albeit a heaven of individual, rational idealism; while Aristotle sought a more ordered, stable understanding of the world. Plato and his followers were greatly influential in early Christian theology, while Aristotle held sway in the Middle Ages, only to be supplanted by Plato again in the Renaissance.

In reality, Aristotle's teachings were a natural progression from Plato's and their particular emphasis was very much influenced by the inconsistencies and omissions which Aristotle saw in his former teacher's body of work. For instance, in his work 'Metaphysics', so named because it appeared after (meta in Greek) his 'Physics', he not only debunks all the pre-Socratics for seeing the prime motivating force behind Creation as something material, but he also takes Plato to task for not addressing the question of this prime motivating force at all.

His concept of God is tied in with his principles of Physics, especially those of motion. For him, God or the Source is the immovable mover, eternal, without magnitude, unalterable, which gives the rest of the material world the impetus to exist. He also describes this God in terms not dissimilar to the Judeo/Christian monotheistic view: 'God is a living being, eternal, most good . . . It thinks of that which is most divine and precious, and it does not change; for change would be for the worse.' This is a far cry from the rational, abstract nature of Socrates' and Plato's search for the Good; the concept of God is now fully seen in completely human, material terms, as opposed to the elemental, material terms of the Pre-Socratics.

As far as the material world is concerned, he is critical of Plato's theory of Forms and the resulting mind/body dualism. From his perspective, matter and form are not separate: it is form which creates things out of matter. In making this not unreasonable distinction between formal and material causes and placing the former above the latter, he makes the regret-table analogy of the female (the material cause) being 'impreg-nated by one copulation' while the male (the formal cause) 'impregnates many females'. How low the Great Goddess has sunk in this rational, male-controlled world!

In a sense, Aristotle has simply created a new dualism by putting the defining quality of form on a pedestal above the expansive nature of pure matter. He goes one step further with his theory of three principles of Form, Privation (of Form) and Matter, where, for instance, in the sphere of night and day, Form is Light, Privation is Darkness and Matter is Air; or, in medicine, Form is Health, Privation is Disease and Matter is the Body. From such a definitive premise, it is basically only one step before one takes away the Matter from this equation and is left with the judgmental dualism of Form and Privation, culminating in its most absolute moral aspect of Good and Evil.

In fact, duality pervades nearly every aspect of Aristotle's philosophy, whose main attributes are the theoretical abso-lutes of logic and proof and his ultimate aim towards the somewhat material ideal of 'living well'. His famous treatises on logic represent a total victory for the extreme duality of the rational mind, as the opposites of truth and falsehood leave no room for shades of grey in the middle or for a way of thinking which in any way validates the intuitive nature of man and the concept of a God which cannot be explained in rational terms.

In his Ethics and Politics, the dualism of good and evil repeatedly comes to the fore, mainly through his attempted definitions as to what good or virtue really is. Like Socrates and Plato, he is devoted to finding the Good, yet he is much less intellectual and more experiential than his predecessors. Like them, he believes that the greatest guide towards Good is one's reason, but he differs as to the means of achieving the knowledge of this ultimate Truth. Instead of rejecting the world of the senses, he sees sensation as being the first rung on the ladder which leads up to the higher levels of thought through the stages of memory, experience, art (which he calls that creative part of man that gives form to matter), theoretical knowledge, and culminating in wisdom.

This more pragmatic philosophy has left behind the mystical and the idealistic and is now materially based. At the heart of it is the search for 'eudaimonia' – best interpreted as happiness or the well-being of the rational mortal. For Aristotle, Good is not to be attained through speculative reasoning, but through virtue, a more practical kind of wisdom which is the sign of a noble character who takes pleasure in doing good. He sees virtue as something which can be taught and which is within the scope of all men, as opposed to intellectual reasoning which is not.

Everything is now firmly on the human plane and it is hardly surprising that Aristotle is better known for his logic and his 'practical sciences' of ethics and politics than for his metaphysics. The essence of his teaching is to dismiss all that is vague and to explain everything in concrete terms; by including God within this framework, he has not only divorced his own philosophical speculation from any intimate connection to the Whole, but has also left the way open to those bands of theologians right through to this present day who have felt the need to define God and man's relationship to 'Him' in rational terms.

By insisting that 'eudaimonia' should be the aim of individual and polis alike, Aristotle formulated the first materialist ethic.

He then goes further to assert that the good of the polis or the state is greater than the good of the individual – a belief in total opposition to the individual conscience and spirit of Socrates. He compares the polis to the human body and the individual to its limbs, thereby denying the importance of an individual's existence and experience outside the structure of the society he lives in. How different from the Egyptian Temple of Man in which the human body is seen to be contained within the whole Universe, rather than the limited earthly realm of the State!

This almost obsessive need to create a stable framework of order is understandable considering the political climate of his day: Athens was decaying around him and he was eventually forced to flee lest he suffer the same fate as Socrates. However, his emphasis on the submission of the individual to the polis or the state – even, in his own words, if the state is a 'bad' state – gives free rein to totalitarianism. Individual expression must be sacrificed for order at any cost.

What is more, within this imposed structure of order exists a further structure of inequality, based on Aristotle's perception of rational capability: 'the slave has no deliberative faculty at all; the woman has, but it is without authority . . . Silence is a woman's glory.' For him, slavery is natural: 'Such a duality exists in living creatures.' There is the ruling mentality, which is the rational; beneath this, there is the slave mentality, which is the passionate. Therefore, democracy, which he sees as the rule of the poor, cannot work.

Aristotle also dismisses Monarchy, Oligarchy and all forms of government except his ideal of Polity: government by a broad 'middle-class', themselves bound by the rule of law which is designed to direct the individual towards a virtuous life. Unlike Plato, he believes that this ruling class should own property – as long as the products of it are used for the common good – and be wealthy, as long as this is natural rather than unnatural wealth (i.e. wealth used for provisions rather than for making more money). He acknowledges that civil strife is most often caused by the desire for personal gain, but offers no solution except the creation of a polity based on Virtue.

It does not take much to see how Aristotle's attempts to define the ideal society and state succeed only in creating a structure which institutionalizes inequality and opens the door to tyranny. In common with other Greeks, he was out of touch with the rest of the world, failing to understand that his beloved polis was a thing of the past, soon to be overtaken by the overwhelming force of Empire, forged by his own former pupil, Alexander the Great.

As with Plato, the immense body of work left by Aristotle was extraordinary for its time. Yet, also in common with Plato, his search to define the Good in rational terms succeeded only in driving mankind further from the natural, intuitive connection to the Source of this Good. While Plato unleashed the rational from the constraints of the spiritual and the material, Aristotle jumbled all the pieces of the jigsaw back together again and embedded the rational in the material. Whether this more human approach to life may seem good or bad from today's perspective is of little relevance. What is important is that the male, rational figure had taken center stage in a totally material, dualistic world.

The course of Western man's evolution had been set.

Alexander died in 323 B.C. and Aristotle died the following year. The arrival of the large scale state, dependent on bureaucracies and presided over by the dictators or oligarchies so scorned by Aristotle, meant the demise of the free polis. Greece left no institutional legacy behind; it was its culture and philosophy which spread its wings of influence throughout the Western world.

The demise of the Athenian ideal also led to the further demise of philosophical inquiry with the 'happiness' of the individual taking center stage over the search for the Good. In this new Hellenic world and thereafter, man's thoughts were turned towards his individual lot in the material world. The search for a connection to a greater Whole, the Source, had long been left behind.

Many philosophical cults arose, each with varying degrees of influence and each reflecting the unsettled world from which they arose. Amongst the most pervasive were the Sceptics who were the natural heirs to the inconclusive nature of the pre-Socratics' and Plato's inquiries, despite the fact that Plato feared the sceptical attitude above all else. In the mind of the Sceptic, if one cannot know anything for certain, one should not even bother searching, but instead aim towards 'ataraxia': peace of mind and freedom from disturbance.

This so-called philosophy, along with Epicureanism which elevates pleasure as the means of attaining this peace of mind, is totally self-centered and finally dismisses any pretension of concern for one's fellow man. The responsibility and active participation encouraged in the ideal polis are seen as a hindrance to this peace of mind. The ideal of Virtue is of no relevance, which illustrates how long virtue really lasts when viewed as a rational concept in a world where there is no spiritual connection to the Whole.

As an extension of the atomists, the Epicureans deny the existence of spirit, of anything that is not material. They see death as the point at which our 'soul atoms' disperse and we no longer feel any sensation – a concept which is not so very different from the atheistic view so prevalent in our world today.

With rare exceptions such as Stoicism, which promoted the harmony of the individual soul with the Universe and insisted that virtue could only be attained when man is indifferent to his material circumstances, the Hellenic Age which existed from Alexander's death to the rise of the Roman Empire saw man more deeply immersed in the quagmire of the self-centered, fearful, material world.

The Hellenic Age's other chief legacy was that education became formalized during this time, but even this strayed far from the ideals of ancient Athens, even of Plato. In opposition to Plato's ideal of the use of dialectics to discover truth, the Sophists' use of rhetoric becomes the focus of intellectual excellence. Its purpose is not to seek the truth, but to foster the mental dexterity which will best equip the student for life. In reality, as Socrates had foreseen, it becomes a competitive game to show who can argue the best, irrespective of truth.

One cannot of course deny that creating a framework for education was a giant step in harnessing the creative forces of man, and the division into subjects such as arithmetic, astronomy, grammar, to name but a few, focused the rational mind in a way which had not been achieved before. However, this system, in addition to dismissing the relevance of the intuitive nature of man, became so analytical by studying old texts and even second-hand commentaries that there was no room for the individual inquiry that had shaped the minds of Socrates, Plato and Aristotle.

When the expansive power of Rome absorbed Greek civilization and culture in the second century B.C., this educational structure became increasingly utilitarian and bred a new class of administrators who were to become the backbone of the Roman Empire – an Empire which was to spread the effects of Greek thought and duality far beyond its own shores.

It seems to have been a long journey from those first philosophical questions on the Ionian coast, but a mere five hundred years have elapsed – infinitesimal in terms of human evolution, but pivotal in terms of the evolution of the mentality which governs our modern world. Furthermore, if one looks back to the 'innocent beginnings' of Greek thought and follows its progress through to the materialistic and self-satisfied mentality which reigned in later years, one can almost see a reflection of the whole span of time from the 'dawn of civilization' in those first settled communities to our present day: the expansion of consciousness passing through many stages until its energy expires, finally bogged down in the quagmire of a purely material world view.

Chapter 6

Christianity: The Religion of Power

When one considers the rise and evolution of the great force of Christianity in the Western world, one soon becomes aware that this religion has much less to do with the teachings of the man after whom it was named than with the powerful influence of the three major civilizations which helped to shape it. The cultural heritage of Judaism, the intellectual heritage of Greece and the institutional heritage of Rome all played a major part in creating the monolithic structure which Christianity had become a mere five hundred years after the death of Christ.

In reality, Christ and his teachings had a great deal more in common with Buddha who had lived five hundred years earlier than with the religion of his name five hundred years later. Both men were miraculously born from a royal line; they both underwent and overcame temptations of the material, physical life leading to a renunciation of old ways and a new life as a wandering teacher performing miracles (i.e. showing their power over the physical world), preaching salvation from within, followed by a small band of disciples.

They both advocated reform within the old religions of Hinduism and Judaism respectively, stressing the personal, spiritual quest rather than formal adherence to law, charity rather that ascetic prohibitions. They repudiated political structures and social, distinctions, renouncing violence and emphasizing the brotherhood of man.

After their deaths, their teachings were spread, but changed in scope by two great empires: in the case of Buddha, the great empire builder Ashoka spread a Buddhism based on the principles of human compassion far beyond the place of the great prophet's life; in the case of Christ, the Roman Emperor Constantine espoused Christianity for political reasons and molded it to his own purposes. After the death of these two emperors, the religions were further structured and diffused within a framework of theology born from the philosophies and cultures of the time and location.

The Christ Consciousness and the Buddha Consciousness are inextricably linked upon this Earth, with one fundamental difference which separates East from West. Whereas the Buddha represents enlightenment through the annihilation of self, the Christ represents the active principle of interaction with the world through love. While Eastern esoteric philosophy preaches disengagement from 'maya', the world of illusion, through meditation and other means of reaching within, the Christ Principle is based on the quest of each individual to find his own Truth through personal experience in the physical world and active participation in the lives of his fellow men.

The essence of Christ the man is that he took spirituality out of the temple and onto the streets so that the masses could find their own spiritual connection to the Source. His essential teachings were that God is within all of us and God is Love; and with this simple dualism of the inner God and the outer, expansive expression of God, He represents duality as the essential, creative force.

Bound with the Truth of Unconditional Love in its three aspects of loving God, the unified Source of one's being, of loving oneself and of loving one's neighbor, are the equal Truths of Humility and Surrender, of washing his disciples' feet and of turning his other cheek. Humility is the understanding that all men are equal, that no one person is superior to another, irrespective of their social or intellectual stature. Surrender is the action of faith, trusting in our intuitive connection to the Source, so that we may follow our individual path to our Highest Good and let go of our fears and our need to control every aspect of our being.

The simplicity of Christ's teachings were in stark contrast

to the Judaic traditions of his upbringing, some of which found their way into Christian theology. In both traditional Judaism and Christianity, we see no God within each and every one of us, but an outside God which, however immanent it is supposed to be in all things, essentially sits in judgment over humanity.

The origin of this outside God goes back to the early heroic age of the Semitic race which was simultaneous with the heroic age of Troy. Unlike the Aryan nomadic tribes which forged their way from the Northern plains, the origin of the Semites was the sparse desert lands of Arabia, from which they gradually settled within the Sumerian city-states, such as Ur, where Abraham spent much of his life.

Although these simple, nomadic folk absorbed all the higher aspects of culture which we associate with this era in Sumeria, their religious beliefs came to stand in total contrast with the Sumerian cyclical view of the Universe, in which the Great Goddess still held sway. Like the nomadic tribes of the North, theirs was an essentially male world, but, unlike their Northern counterparts, theirs came to be an exclusive male God which vengefully destroyed all opposition.

The difference between this one omnipotent God of the Semites and the panoply of humanized Greek gods which absorbed the many local gods and goddesses in their path reflects the fundamental contrast between the Jewish rigid and somewhat fatalistic view of the world and the Greek mentality of creative, human activity. The Greek world was essentially expansive and universal; the Semitic world was essentially contractive and ethnocentric.

The first evidence of an exclusively Semitic mythology is the Poem of Creation in which the victory of the Babylonian male god Marduk over the female goddess Tiamat is glorified. This move towards an exclusive male god,* which is also evident in the adoption of the Western Semite god Yahweh, must be seen in terms of the continuous conflict which was at the time taking place within the whole area of Mesopotamia. The period

---

*Despite the adoption of a male god, Jewish history is full of larger than life female figures, and, to this day, Jewish women rule the home and the family – evidence that the female energy can never be truly suppressed.

after 2000 B.C. was the era of Semitic expansion throughout the ancient civilization of Sumeria and beyond, as far as the Mediterranean Sea. The Old Testament was the idealized chronicle of a particular Semitic tribe's history, and the 'God' within it was no more than the tribal, politically motivated god of the Semitic race – a necessary, outer focus of tribal unity within a world of constant flux.

Because this divine principle emanated from a specific race, as opposed to an individual prophet such as Christ or Buddha, its emphasis would always be of a particularly social and political nature, and the whole concept of each individual finding his own God within would pose a threat to the cohesion and unity of the race as a whole. The ultimate result of this is a religion which raises the particular race up as a 'chosen people' above all others and which is firmly bound by the rule of Law, perceived as emanating from a Higher Being called God and not in its initial stages, open to individual interpretation. The insistence on the Creation of Man as historical fact rather than symbol, as discussed in the first chapter of this book, is an extension of this mentality.

This tendency was formalized around 450 B.C. when, under the tolerant eye of Persian rule, the great Jewish patriarch Nehemiah established a theocracy of religious uniformity based on written law – just in time to create a base of orthodoxy and exclusiveness for the Jewish race as it faced the great diaspora which began at the end of the fourth century B.C.

It was essentially this elitism and rigidity which made the conflict between the Jewish religious establishment and the individual spirit of Christ so inevitable – and, after the death of Christ, it was Judaic orthodoxy that prevailed once again. When one looks at the fundamental similarities between Judaism and Christianity, they have more to do with structure and hierarchy than spiritual content. The basic precept of a code of righteousness according to law, where the righteous go to heaven and the evil go to hell, together with the unquestioned role of religious leaders and their interpretation of this 'moral' doctrine – all this leads straight into the hands of those who choose to use religion for their own power, which is exactly what Jesus spent his life fighting against.

But, most important of all, it is the spirit of Christ's teachings which is lost. The God Within, the power of Love and the individual's quest to find his own inner path are suffocated at birth by the mentality which believes in an omnipotent, separate Creator and which fears the creative power of the individual, of woman and of sexuality.

Within this environment, it is with the rise of a Christian theology that Greek influence comes to the fore and the one principal figure who brings the Greek and Judaic culture together in the formation of Christianity is Saint Paul. Despite his supposed revelation on the road to Damascus, Paul of Tarsus was and essentially remained a Hellenized Jew.

Like many Jews of his class, Paul had a great deal of contact with Hellenic education, philosophy and culture, so it is no wonder that he interpreted Christ's teachings in his own individual way. He retained the Judaic way of seeing an immanent God 'in the midst of us' rather than within us, and combined this with the typically Greek mentality of seeing Christ in human terms, with the individual aspects of His life and personality holding sway over the spiritual consciousness which He personified.

However, it was through the expansive nature of Greek culture that Paul had the greatest impact on Christianity. He was no Jew in the sense of seeing religion in ethnocentric terms (although he did spread the Judaic idea of an exclusive God who favored only those who worshipped Him); he was very Greek in his outlook in that he preached the universality of his and Christ's teachings, expanding the message of Christ far beyond the area in which the man Jesus worked and lived.

The great cross-fertilization of Christianity with other cultures occurred most strongly in the Egyptian city of Alexandria, which was, in the time after Christ's death, a melting pot of all races and beliefs, from native Egyptian to Jewish, Persian, Greek and Christian. In Egypt itself, Christianity was tolerated as one of many religious cults and was, in its early stages, particularly favored because of the many similarities to Egyptian beliefs, in particular those of resurrection and reincarnation. In addition, with the closing of many temples in Egypt, the individual quest of the gnostics had come to the fore and Christ's teachings were naturally embraced by them.

However, within this teeming city of Alexandria, it was the

intellectual climate of Hellenistic culture which had the most profound influence on Christianity. In the first century A.D., Philo, a practicing Jew strongly influenced by Greek thought, put forward the idea that one could attain revelation through the 'Logos' – literally translated as the Word, but more broadly representing the rational mind. This concept had a major influence on the Hellenized Christians of his day and opened up the link in the Christian mind between the inner knowledge of feeling God as taught by Christ and the rational knowledge of the Greek mind.

It is with the Platonists that this connection becomes firmly established, and the subsequent, inevitable creation of a theology based on intellect soon raised the rational quest for God above the inner revelation of Christ. In defining God in the terms of Plato's Good, the so-called middle-Platonists saw God as a transcendent reality which was independent of the world of our senses and which could only be reached through philosophical inquiry. Not only does this once more separate God from man in a much more theistic way than Plato himself would have allowed, but it firmly establishes within Christian thought the supremacy of the mind and spirit over the body.

The Neo-Platonists revised this by arguing that the Source of reality was not a supreme being or intellect, but a Oneness or Good beyond our knowing. But then, Plotinus, their most famous philosopher, went further and tried to rationalize the ancient Trinity of Egypt, (of course, removing from it the female, creative principle!), by adding to this unknowable Oneness the intellectual principle of self-awareness in man, (which he saw in terms of the 'Nous' of Anaxagoras), and the Soul, which was the intermediary between the Nous and the material world. The confused, masculine Trinity of the Father, the Son, the Holy Ghost which Christianity adopted is a direct result of this absurd game of trying to define the indefinable.

Platonism was of course a genuine attempt, in a typically Greek way, to create a belief in the goodness of the world as an image of divine perfection. However, needless to say, this rational inquiry squeezes the intuitive, spiritual connection to the Source out of religious experience and serves merely to create a framework of theology which can readily be turned into dogma.

Whatever influence Jewish and Greek thought had on Christianity, it would have remained very much a local religion without the might of Rome behind it. In its early years, Christianity was plagued by fanatical cults and by persecution, in particular by the Roman Emperor Diocletian, but its moment arrived with the renowned 'conversion' of Constantine the Great.

This event was the most momentous in the history of Christianity, for, by embracing it, Constantine destroyed any basic link there was with the teachings of Christ. By choosing to espouse and glorify Christianity for political reasons, he totally absorbed it into the structure of the Roman State. Where Christ had taught humility and surrender, turning the other cheek and loving His enemies, Constantine raised himself up as the great warrior, killing the enemies of a God which was now made manifest in imperial power and wealth.

The final blow came at the Council of Niceae which Constantine called in 325 A.D., supposedly to deal with a theological debate concerning the Trinity but in reality to impose his authority on his newly adopted religion. At this and subsequent councils, the formalized creed and dogma of Christianity was set in stone and the power of Church and State were launched on their paths of interdependence and conflict which were to endure for centuries.

After the Council of Niceae, reincarnation, gnosticism and anything which was perceived as encouraging the individual search for enlightenment were proscribed as acts of heresy. Even the theological debate which had taken place in Hellenistic times fell under the same axe, as it too was perceived as a threat to the order and stability of the State. The Universal Authority was now the secular, material power of the State, and any spiritual consciousness had to be dedicated to it or else be suppressed and destroyed.*

However, after the death of Constantine, the Roman Empire began to break up and its power gradually faded. As it did, the Church, which had been institutionalized by Constantine and

---

*This is in evidence in the formalization of ritual, where its more 'ecstatic' (and therefore disruptive) elements were suppressed in favor of an ordered ceremony where the presence of Christ was identified with substance (i.e. bread and wine) as opposed to spirit.

had assumed the imperial colors, grew in power to such an extent that Emperor Theodosius, who, despite the fact that he imposed religious orthodoxy even more forcefully than his predecessor Constantine had done fifty years earlier, still had to do penance to the Archbishop of Milan after offending him in some matter.

From this point on, the Church imitated the State in every way, living in palaces, raising armies and assuming wealth and property as its right and its hallmark. No longer did its leaders follow the words of Christ: 'Blessed are the poor, for theirs is the kingdom of God.' Instead, the Church hierarchy raised themselves above the common folk and abused other words to justify a social structure of order and power: 'What God has joined together, let not man put asunder.'

So it was that the Judaic, Greek and Roman cultural heritages combined to create in Christianity the very antithesis of Christ's teachings. Where Christ taught the God Within, Christianity put forward a view of a separate God, immanent in the ridiculously confusing Trinity of Father, Son and Holy Ghost; where Christ brought spirituality out of the temple and directly into the lives of the common people, Christianity squeezed it back into the confines of the church; while Christ renounced the trappings of the material world, the Christian hierarchy made itself fat by exploiting the masses; where Christ preached love, humility and surrender, the Christian church spread war, arrogance and control. The list is endless.

Within this new order of power, duality abounded and fed itself. The notion of Sin and the dualisms of Good and Evil, of Heaven and Earth, with the implication that one would be rewarded in Heaven if one suffered on Earth, were perfect implements for keeping the masses in their place. The dualism of Church and State ultimately became an illusion as they each sought after the same goal of material power. The Spirit and the Flesh were made irreconcilable by a mentality which suppressed the female energy and feared the uncontrollable forces of sexuality. And, more than anything, it was the Material which had come to dominate and stifle the Spiritual.

And what of the Christ Consciousness? Why was the man Jesus born, if all his teachings were to be overturned and suppressed?

The answer to this is that, with the birth and the death of Jesus, the Christ Consciousness was rooted on the Earth. The hierarchy of power perverted it, yet, ever since His time to this very day, there have been shining examples both within and outside the Christian church of those who have tried to live their lives according to the principles of Christ. The individual has had to find out for himself or herself what Truth is, while the old structure of power, in whatever form it exists, will continue on its own, rigid path until it comes face to face with a force it cannot control: the second coming of the Christ – not in the old-fashioned view of the 'Son of God' coming down from Heaven to save us, but with the true Christ Consciousness being carried in the hearts and minds of the many who will combine their individual powers to create the change which is necessary for mankind to move ahead to the next stage in our evolution as conscious beings.

Chapter 7

The Middle Ages and the Stirring of the Individual

There is an inherent dualism in the period from the fall of Rome to the beginning of the Renaissance: the external history and the internal growth of Western man.

On the one hand, there is what we read in the history books: the splitting of the Roman Empire into East and West; the so-called Dark Ages following the barbaric invasions from the North; the continuous battle for supremacy between Church and State and the seemingly universal need to create order at all costs by rigid control of the masses, suppressing any threat to orthodoxy or to the status quo of the ruling class; the growth of feudalism; the lack of any original philosophical thought with scholasticism in the hands of a clergy which merely looks backwards to the interpretation of old ideas – all of these point to a period of regression or, at best, stagnation.

On the other hand, there is the power of the masses which becomes manifest with the breakdown of order in the Dark Ages. The 'barbaric' tribes which swept down from the North and overwhelmed the decaying Western Roman Empire were not constrained by the external structures and complex hierarchies of 'civilized' society. Theirs was a world which had more recently thrown off the yoke of the Universal Authority of the Group; unlike their Southern enemies who had attempted to create a civilization built on a foundation of reason, they were less capable of separating themselves from their impulses and therefore, instead of being able to identify them and take responsibility for them, they had a greater tendency to be overwhelmed by them.

Within these Northern tribes, there was greater individual expression than was permitted in the Roman Empire in which the desires of the individual were always subsidiary to the greater order of the State. What is more, these less educated and 'irrational' Northern races were much closer to the Earth and to the pagan traditions of earlier times than the civilization they overran and ultimately absorbed. Despite the fact that an external order eventually prevailed in the West during the Middle Ages, the temporary supremacy of Northern unbridled energy and imagination left a lasting impact on the inner psyche of Western man.

On an external plane, however, the main result of the turmoil of the Dark Ages was the compulsive need to create and maintain a structure of order and control at all costs – and it was Christianity which became the unifying force of this new order, maintaining the Latin language of the Imperial past as a means of bringing together the diverse cultures and languages which came under its dominion.

In the sixth century, Clovis of the Franks annihilated his rivals, but reconciled the Gallo-Roman population by embracing the Christian faith. On Christmas Day 800 A.D., Charlemagne was crowned Emperor by the Pope of Rome, beginning the Holy Roman Empire of the German Nation, which, after his death, became immersed in the continuous struggle between the secular power of the Emperor and the religious power of the Pope.

Underneath all of this, there emerged the new hierarchy of feudalism, a mutual system of obligations centered around land granted to warriors in return for services to leaders such as Charlemagne. As the central authority of the Emperor and the Church declined due to their constant in-fighting, this new class of landowners began to look to their own power, becoming independent rulers over a powerless class of tenants who now owed them allegiance and service in war.

When these feudal overlords were not fighting invaders, they were constantly fighting amongst themselves, creating a completely ego- and male-dominated world in which greed and lust for power predominated. It was an era of the most violent and uncontrolled impulses, and it was also an age when the oligarchy lost its absolute monopoly of power and the common man had his first taste of being able to assert his own power and have dominion over others – not a pretty picture, but a necessary part of man's evolution.

It was therefore hardly surprising that the religious establishment felt a need to keep control and maintain order at all costs. In such an atmosphere of flux and change with old barriers being constantly broken down, stability was the main aim of the Christian hierarchy. Any 'heresy' was brutally crushed; scholastic knowledge was preserved and interpreted in a conservative and derivative manner so as not to create any doubt or new ideas which could threaten the established order.

Even in the twelfth century, when the West once more came into contact with the ancient Greek philosophers whose works had been preserved by the Eastern Roman Empire of Byzantium and by the expanding Moslem Arab world, Christian scholars and theologians borrowed only small portions of their writings in order to support their own ends.

The most famous and influential of all of these was Thomas Aquinas who interpreted Aristotle's metaphysical teachings in his own way to support his theory of the dualism of Reason and Revelation, whereby Reason, combined with the experience of the senses, leads to Rational Knowledge, and Revelation, whose scope included those elements such as the Trinity and Resurrection which lay beyond the scope of reason, leads to Faith.

This dualism in the sphere of knowledge had a profound influence on Western thought once Thomas's teachings were embraced by the Christian Church after his death. Although he asserted that there was no conflict between the two, he implied that faith was required before rational knowledge was pursued, a fact which did not prevent him from maintaining that the existence of God could be proved in rational terms – something which he and his many successors have palpably failed to do.

With Plato and Aristotle, the search for the Good lay behind every aspect of their philosophical inquiry; the fundamental result of Thomas Aquinas's essential division between

Faith and Rational Knowledge was that Revelation came to be perceived as the exclusive realm of religion and theology, while Reason was the base for philosophical inquiry and the blossoming field of natural sciences. Although it freed scientific study from the constraints of theology, this absolute division also ensured that research into the spiritual and physical planes of existence came to be perceived as irreconcilable. The later conflict between Galileo and the Church was an inevitable consequence of this, just as was the Newtonian view of physics which sees the Universe in purely material terms.

Thomas Aquinas's political writings were equally espoused by the Church, which is hardly surprising considering that their primary emphasis is on the maintenance of an order whose authority comes directly from God. The aim of the individual should not be to live a virtuous life as an end in itself, but to attain divine fruition by means of a virtuous life, which can only be truly guided by the divine government of the Pope in whom spiritual and secular powers are joined together. What is more, inferiors must always obey superiors in order to maintain order within human society, the only justification for revolt being if one is ruled by a heretic!

In the twelfth century, this is exactly the kind of order which had been established. It was the era of the great cathedrals, of a wealthy Church hierarchy ruling as the human embodiment of divine will over the poor masses – reflecting a state of power and control which was simultaneously occurring throughout the world, with the dominance of the Mongols in China and Russia, of Islam in India and of the Inca and Aztec Empires at the height of their oppression in South and Central America.

This is the era which Jung saw as the mid-point of the Piscean Age when the dualism of the Christ and Anti-Christ was at its most extreme state, with the majority of those forces which purported to represent Christ acting out the antithesis of His teachings, while the Christ Consciousness itself manifested in less ostentatious ways and more isolated places.

The obvious groups within the Christian Church which fall into the latter category are the Dominican and Franciscan orders of monks who, before they too became institutionalized, mixed with and ministered to the poor, teaching them their own spiritual worth. However, they were a still, small voice within the overwhelming might of the Church, and, therefore, in order to uncover the vital forces which were the true standard-bearers of the Christ Consciousness of enlightenment through individual quest and love, we must look to the outer fringes of the 'Christian' empire, where the ancient, native traditions still survived and even flourished.

In the northern islands of Britain and Ireland, there was an uninterrupted line of so-called pagan traditions in which the Great Goddess and Mother Earth prevailed. The initial Roman occupation had merely been temporary and it was only after the Synod of Whitby* in 664 A.D. that the native cults in Britain were forced underground by the persecution of the exclusive Christian religion.

All along the Atlantic coast, from Spain to Scotland, there had existed a distinct civilization which has been dated by modern archaeology as being antecedent to the flowering of civilization in the Near East. Mounds have been found which date back as far as 5000 B.C. and which were not only used for burial but were also aligned with the mid-summer sun, suggesting some kind of ceremonial function. Myths of an ancient sea-faring folk, escaping the destruction of their own civilization (Atlantis) of course abound along this area of the Western seaboard.

Throughout Britain and Ireland, there still can be seen a great number of stone circles, established following specific geometric patterns on sites with renowned dynamic qualities and all connected along a series of 'ley lines' which spread right across the country. The ritual associated with these circles was closely tied in with the fluctuating seasons and was presided over by a priesthood which was responsible for maintaining the harmony of this early man with Nature, the Earth and the Universe.

The most well known of all these stone circles is of course Stonehenge. The first evidence of building on this site goes back to 3000 B.C., although the final structure (which we can imagine from the existing ruins) was not completed until a thousand years later, built from stone brought in from Wales almost a hundred miles away. Like the Pyramids and other

---

*This is where religious orthodoxy finally triumphed in Britain over the more fluid elements of the Celtic Church.

ancient megalithic structures, Stonehenge was a temple which
reflected the magnitude of the Cosmos with its geometric
structure in complete alignment with the movement of the
sun and the moon, the male and female principles.

What is not known for sure is who built this amazing monu-
ment – whether it was the descendants of the earlier civilization
from the West or the so-called Celts who migrated to Britain
from the South and are believed by some to have originated
from the priestly caste of ancient Sumeria. What we do know
for sure, however, is that, when Julius Caesar invaded Britain in
55 B.C., there already existed a flourishing and densely popu-
lated farm culture, the unifying force of which was the priestly
caste of the Druids.

By all accounts, the Druid was a remarkable, sacred figure
who had total spiritual and temporal authority, even over the
individual tribal chiefs. The Druid represented the merging
of the physical and spiritual planes: on the one hand, he
was a healer and a judge who presided over any conflict or
disagreement; on the other hand, his knowledge of astronomy and ritual brought the community as a whole in touch
with the universal energies of the Source. He was particularly
renowned as a Bard, who, through the sacred knowledge of
breath and vibration, used poetry and song to heighten the
frequency of consciousness within his community.

The power of the Druid ultimately waned, but many of the
pagan traditions were actively kept alive in the early Celtic
Christian Church, and, even after the Synod of Whitby, the
mysteries of the old religion were practiced in secret. Even
as late as the twelfth century, one of the great works of medieval literature appeared: *Vita Merlini* (*The Life of Merlin*), written
by Geoffrey of Monmouth, a man who was evidently equally
learned in both the pagan and Christian traditions.

Merlin is the most powerful, partly mythical, partly historical
figure to come down to us from the era when the old religion
and connection to the vital spirits of the Earth were still practiced. He is portrayed as living during the heroic age of Britain
after the departure of the Romans, when the previous tribal
culture had disintegrated to be replaced by princely states.

During this era of turmoil, he stands out as a remarkable symbol of 'Unity through Human Experience' and can be compared
as the Christ in a more primitive, nature-connected state when

the conscious emerged from the well of the unconscious. He is – in the tradition of Pan, Odin, Lug from other cultures – the Trickster, the amoral, carnal, Shaman/Lord of the Forests – the Horned Beast representing the uncontrollable forces of the individual, portrayed by the Christian church as the Devil. He alternates between insanity and absolute clarity, melding the conscious and unconscious worlds together through the intensity of suffering and human emotion, finally to emerge in an enlightened state. His world is the very antithesis of the cold world of ethical, judgmental duality!

Each page of *The Life of Merlin* is rife with the most powerful symbolism. It starts with Merlin's descent into madness as he watches a battle between two opposing tribes, representing the polarity of the duality of the material world. He retreats to the Forest (the depth of the subconscious and the connection to the Earth) and utters his Winter Lament, in which the season of Winter symbolizes the stillness of going within, getting in touch with the subconscious in order to realize the conscious. When Spring arrives, he is wakened by the sound of music (i.e. clarity restored by pure harmony) and is reminded of his wife Guendolena, harmonizing the male and female principles within himself. He is lured back and kept against his will at the court of King Rhydderich, who, though a good man, represents the temptation of the material world and whose ultimate death releases Merlin from the attachments it represents. After many events, including his highly symbolic foretelling of a threefold death by falling, hanging and drowning (a version of the universal myth of the sacrificed innocent god, reconciling through his death the four separate elements of fire, air, water and earth), Merlin is finally healed at a fountain (the universal energies of the Goddess) and transfers his power of prophecy to his sister before retiring from the world.

Inherent within the symbolism of this story is the threefold aspect of both man and woman, which is an extension of the Trinity of the ancient mysteries. Merlin himself passes through the three stages: the first stage of the innocent youth who, through his primal spiritual link with the Source, utters prophecies; the middle stage of the mature man who lives in the duality of the material world and, through the conflict and pain of human experience, develops to the final stage of the wise old man who returns to the unity of a spiritual life.

The threefold aspects of woman are represented by three different figures in The Life of Merlin. His sister Ganieda represents the purity of non-sensual love and unchanging, gentle wisdom; his wife Guendolena embodies the polarity of sexual energy and fertility in the female principle of sensual love and motherhood; finally, there appears at the end of the tale a shady old woman selling poisonous apples, representing the death crone or shape-changer, the archetypal female figure with mysterious powers over life and death, breaking down the old and transforming it into the new.

What is remarkable about the retelling and popularity of this archetypal myth at the height of the 'Christian age' is that it must have presupposed a certain knowledge of the symbols of the ancient, pagan religion. Here in the North, despite the apparent supremacy of the Christian establishment, its distance from the religious center of Rome ensured that the old ways were not stamped out. The elemental energies of the individual and his connection to the Earth and the greater Whole existed in a way which only survived in pockets in the South where the individual was subjugated not only to the State, but also to a rational theology which negated physical experience as a path to spiritual fulfillment.

However, despite the Northern location of the Merlin story, Merlin himself was also part of other traditions which spread throughout Western Europe. As everyone knows, Merlin figures strongly in the Arthurian legends, which include two of the most powerful elements of the medieval quest for personal spiritual fulfillment: the Courtly Love of Lancelot and Guenevere and the Quest for the Holy Grail.

The late medieval world was one of masculine control. There was the feudal hierarchy of landowner, knight and vassal and there was the power of the Church with a similarly rigid structure. In both hierarchies, woman was on the very lowest rung, being denied to those who were devoted to the Christian religion and being treated as mere chattel for the man in the material world where marriage was simply another means for the Church to maintain social order. And yet, however much the female principle may have been suppressed within the hierarchy of control her elemental power is too strong not to assert itself in other ways.

With the relative stability of the late Middle Ages, there began a much deeper interchange of cultures between the West and the Byzantine and Arab Empires. The effect on scholasticism has already been noted, but of equal and more positive effect was the cross-fertilization of mystical traditions. Under the guise of the 'true Christian faith', the Roman Church had suppressed any threat to orthodoxy, driving native cults underground; yet, contact with the Arab world, in particular with the Kabbalah and Sufism, the mystical elements of Judaism and Islam respectively, stimulated a gradual re-awakening of pagan traditions and, with it, a reassertion of the female principle.

This influence was probably strongest in the South of France, where, influenced by the Sufi belief in earthly love as a means of reaching spiritual perfection, the renowned Troubadors raised Woman and the divine principle of Love to an elevated plane never before experienced in this male dominated world. Within a short period of time, this melding of cultures created its own tradition of epics, its own code of chivalry and even the specialized language: 'langue d'oc'.

The reputed father of the Troubadour tradition, Guillaume IX, grandfather of the much lauded Eleanor of Aquitaine, was as bawdy a character as any creation of Chaucer, and yet the tradition of the Troubadour quickly evolved into a very special kind of spiritual/physical love which could never be consummated because of the inferior rank of the suitor. This unattainable female figure in her symbolic ivory tower looked down to the forlorn figure of the simple knight – she combined a pure, physical beauty with an ennobling quality which went deep into the very heart of her admirer. Like a goddess, she led him on an inner journey of transformation towards a oneness with his own receptive, intuitive, feminine nature, expressed in the poetry and music of his love songs.

This was also the era that the cult of the Virgin Mary began to sweep through the Christian world – the first time since the Council of Nicaea that the female principle had been granted some recognition in the male dominated world of the Christian Church.

Of course, one cannot fail to be aware that both Courtly Love and the worship of the Virgin Mary retained a purity, devoid of sexuality, which was acceptable to the Church hierarchy.

On the Continent of Europe, any devotion to the Goddess in all her creative/destructive power was practiced in secret for fear of persecution as heresy by the Inquisition. Likewise, sexual union between man and woman could be celebrated in the bawdy tales of the day, but could not be acknowledged as a path towards spiritual growth, such as it was perceived in the less orthodox traditions which had begun to filter through from the East.

From these same traditions, originating in the Middle East, came the legend of the 'Graal', which was gradually Christianized in Western Europe and became known as The Holy Grail. The popularity of the Grail Romance reached its height in the late 12th and early 13th century, the first written down version of it being attributed to Chrétien de Troyes in France, although it soon spread and was integrated into legends of Germany, Britain and beyond.

Within the Grail story are many of the elements of the Merlin legend, but, in this case, the central character of the 'innocent' knight is much more the mortal ideal of the striving hero, combining an outer quest with an inner search, integrating the physical with the spiritual. Although its origin and symbolism go far back to the ancient Mystery Schools of pre-Christian times, this myth is very much a Western story of engagement with the world through experiences of the senses as opposed to the Eastern transformation through asceticism and meditation.

Other elements and characters which appear in various combinations in all the different versions of the story are a King, a Maiden, the Powers of Life and Death, a Hermit and certain symbols, the chief among them being the Cup and the Lance. On the surface, the object of the Grail Quest was to restore the King to health and thereby restore fertility to his land, implying a connection to the vegetation/fertility rights of old.

Chrétien de Troyes' hero, Perceval, is portrayed as an ideal of purity, but not the sterile purity of the unsexual Galahad in Mallory's later sanitized, Christian telling of the story in *Morte d'Arthur*. Perceval is a simple, uncorrupted, noble son of Nature, even a Fool, who is swept along his individual path of spontaneous experience, often sexual, with no inbuilt fears of the subconscious or of the 'dark' female mysteries. He surrenders to fate and his inner search has little to do with finding the right answer, as would be the ideal for the rational Greek mind; the culmination of his personal quest comes with his asking the right question – in other words, the quest is open ended without any particular, specific goal and is fulfilled quite simply by following one's individual path of experience with an open, inquiring mind.

The unity of the material and spiritual world is represented by the Grail itself. In some traditions, it is seen as Christ's Chalice at the Last Supper, or, in others, as the Philosopher's Stone of alchemical heritage by which 'base matter' (i.e. primal, corruptible energy) is sublimated into gold (i.e. pure, incorruptible essence), the one adding greater power to the other. But, more than anything, the Grail is the search itself, the Quest for the Eternal, the willingness to delve deep into the inner realms of the subconscious and fuse it with the conscious world.

One of the most powerful images of the Quest for the Grail is that of the Fisher King, lying for years wounded by a spear in the thighs, or more to the point, in the genitals. Here, with his blood and life force seeping out, lies the wounded male principle which has ruled the Western world for over a millennium. Around him is desert, representing the spiritual desolation caused by the denial of the female principle and the sexual energy which brings union in the spiritual and physical planes. Here, we see again the Jungian image of the crisis point in the Age of Pisces (the *Fisher* King), together with the symbol of the Spear, the same archetypal weapon used to kill not only Christ on the cross, but also such Nordic mythological figures of higher consciousness as Odin and Lug.

What brings healing to the Fisher King is the appearance of Perceval, the innocent Fool who has followed his own path of mortal experience in order to reach this culmination of asking the Question of the Fisher King. It is the simple, sensual man coming face to face with the desiccated energy of the controlling force which had kept the elemental power of the masses in check for hundreds of years.

All of these medieval myths look forward to the new age of the individual, where the old hierarchy begins to crumble and the masses begin their slow climb out of oppression. What they all have in common are uncomplicated heroes who are children of Nature, unrestrained by the limits imposed by the laws and strictures of a colder world dominated by the rational mind. The emphasis here is on the personal quest for spiritual growth and Unity through an exploration rather than a denial of the world of the senses and the emotions – something which would have been inconceivable to the Greek philosophers and the Christian theologians who had succeeded in driving a wedge between the physical and spiritual worlds.

Chapter 8

Renaissance, Reformation and Rationalism

However strong this individual yearning for inner spiritual fulfill-ment may have been during the late Middle Ages, it was engulfed by a much more powerful force which holds sway within the minds of men to this very day: the urge to improve one's material condition.

Once more, this time in the fourteenth century, there occurred in the evolution of Western man a hiatus which was to launch him on yet another new path. A combina-tion of the Black Death, which wiped out a third of the population of Europe, and the economic collapse of the monarchies and the empires, which had extended them-selves beyond their means, left the way open for the emergence in strength of the new merchant class which had been steadily growing in stature during the late Middle Ages.

As feudalism, the Church and the Empire all began to lose control over their populations and over their finances, the merchants were the natural heirs. No longer did wealth come from power; it was now wealth which produced power, from the trading cities of Northern Italy to the commercial and banking capitals of Germany and the low countries. With the crumbling of the old structures, it is money which to this day rules the world – a scenario which Aristotle so vehemently

scorned, but to whose creation he had unwittingly contributed. The understandable desire to create a better physical
existence submerges the deeper yearning for a spiritual connection to the Source.

What Aristotle called 'unnatural money' (money to make
more money, as opposed to money as a medium of exchange
for provisions) now held sway. With banks creating debt
through money lending with interest, the men behind them
exerted a control which to this day has not been broken.
Material greed ruled merchants and the common man, and
this ethic was soon rooted in the New World by Columbus
and all who followed him, destroying the dignity and cultural
traditions of the native people they overwhelmed.

It is also from this point on that any philosophical thought
confines itself almost completely to the material world, and
any attempt to look into the spiritual life of man and beyond is
constrained by a rational outlook which becomes increasingly
insistent on empirical proof. Rarely do we see glimpses of the
individual quest for the Holy Grail – even such movements
as the Reformation, which arose out of a genuine desire for
a more personal, spiritual connection to God, soon became
submerged in rationalist dogma and were then swept away
in the tide of political opportunism.

This all arises naturally from the powerful influence of
Thomas Aquinas's revelation/reason dualism which frees
philosophy from theology, leaving spiritual inquiry in the
hands of conservative scholars of orthodox religion, few of
whom had the capacity to delve into their personal, inner
being. In contrast with this rigidity and stagnation on the
spiritual plane, the material world of science, politics and
the new concept of 'social philosophy' embraced by the
Humanists exploded any restraints that had held them back
in the Middle Ages and opened the way for a veritable New
Age of creativity.

One of the essential motivating forces of the Renaissance
was the rediscovery of the ancient texts in their entirety, in
particular those of Aristotle and Plato. Whereas the medieval
scholars had picked out little pieces which they subtly used to
reinforce pre-existent ideas, the re-emergence of the political
and social works of Plato and Aristotle created a fervor of new
ideas, as Man was drawn back into center stage after centuries

dominated by the medieval obsession with the nature of the external God which they worshipped.

And, of course, the essential Renaissance spirit was personified by such giants as Leonardo da Vinci and Michelangelo: artist, scientist, architect, poet, freethinker all wrapped up in one individual. Within these extraordinary men, the spiritual and physical were united in art in the broadest Aristoltelian sense of the word: bringing form and beauty and knowledge together out of the Whole of the Universe.

The melding of great scientific and artistic creativity within the formidable minds of these few geniuses of the Renaissance was a flourishing of inner power which has barely been harnessed within one single individual ever since. This amazing eruption of imagination and invention was the high point of unified human creativity, for a sense of spirit and awe of the Universe were simultaneously expressed in art, which we today associate with the intuitive mind, and in science, which we connect with the rational mind.

On a purely creative level, therefore, these Renaissance men represent a pinnacle of unified human achievement from which man has since fallen. The continuous flux and seeming disorder of the Middle Ages had produced an environment in which, once the old structures of power were swept aside, these special individuals were able to balance their rational and intuitive natures, combining ancient knowledge with the wealth of human experience. The results of just these few men bringing these aspects of duality into unity are there for us all to see. Just imagine what could be achieved if this energy was brought together in our own times!

However, this remarkable balance and universality was but a fleeting moment, as the rational once more took hold – this time, in the form which has largely been responsible for man's rapid evolution on the material plane: Specialization. From this point on, with few exceptions, we see artists, scientists, theologians, poets, philosophers, etc. excelling in their own fields, influencing their own specific media, but never again to such a degree bringing the whole panoply of creativity together as one.

At the high point of the Italian Renaissance, the great thinkers – scientists and artists alike – turned away from the confused, artificially complex theology of the Middle Ages and returned to the mathematical traditions of Pythagoras and Plato, enabling the idea of the mathematical structure of the Universe to bring a unity into all forms of creative expression: in art and architecture returning to the idea of the harmony of the Infinite Source, latent since Ancient Egypt and Greece; and in science fuelling the desire to find the key to the Universe, from the Heliocentric theory of Copernicus to the inspirational theories of Kepler and Galileo.

And yet, as we well know, in 1633, Galileo was forced by the ecclesiastical authorities to recant and this brief flurry of individual speculation was once again swamped by the powers in whose interest it lay to maintain the status quo. Just as the innocent speculation of the pre-Socratics in early Greece ultimately degenerated to the cynical attitude of those whose 'philosophical' goal was to cope the best they could – so it was that the originality, and most important of all, the fluidity of the great Renaissance figures were superseded by the rigidity of lesser beings rooted in the material world.

In the field of science, even one of the most heralded figures, Isaac Newton, who lived only half a century after the 'disgrace' of Galileo, created laws which, however original they were for his time, were so rigid and fixed in their view of the physical world that it is only in this century that their grip has been loosened to open the way up for a more flexible, all-encompassing view of the Universe as a whole.

In the spiritual field, the Catholic Church still maintained its authority in the South and the great hope for a return to an individual connection with God devoid of all dogma lay in the North where the excesses of the Catholic hierarchy had begun to weaken its hold over the people. Northern Europe had itself experienced its own artistic Renaissance with such artists as Bosch, Dürer and Grunewald, who demonstrated a much more impulsive, elemental, albeit at times somewhat macabre explosion of imagination than the more classical inspiration of the South.

This was a popular expression of artistic liberty less subject to the Catholic dogma and control which reigned even during the Renaissance in Italy and it was a natural progression that Erasmus's vision of man standing in direct relation to God would appeal to this freer Northern imagination, sweeping away theology as being superfluous to individual, spiritual experience. The ideals of the Reformation emanated from that rebellious part of the Northern mentality which had never truly submitted to being told what and how to worship.

Yet, it happened to be that the most famous and influential champion of this potentially great spiritual movement was not a man who saw individual freedom as paramount. Despite his courage in standing up to the Catholic Church, Martin Luther was a deeply conservative man, in general respectful of authority, who even condemned the peasant revolts of his time because of his obsession with maintaining order. With him at the helm and with the subsequent influence of the even more cold, logical, puritanical Calvin, this new religion became static and rigid even before it had chance to flow.

Of course, the less rigid Protestants certainly emphasized an individual connection to God and a freer sense of personal responsibility, just as certain Catholics have throughout history done great deeds of individual conscience. Sadly, though, what remained of the Protestant faith after it had been politicized by the Germanic princes rebelling against the authority of Rome was a religion which, in devotion, was much poorer than the one it had superseded. Although Roman Catholicism, with its emphasis on dogma and control, squeezed the spirit out of religion, its rituals at least allowed for an emotional connection with God. The Protestant religion, once it too became institutionalized, turned its back on the free, individual expression of its origin and assumed the other extreme of the Germanic character: cold discipline, obedience and dry intellect.

This dry intellect was particularly in evidence in the now very distinct discipline of philosophy. René Descartes, (1596–1650), so-called father of modern philosophy whose renowned 'logic' of 'I think, therefore I am' placed rational thought on a pedestal from which it has not yet fallen, was actually a Catholic, as opposed to the predominately Protestant philosophers who followed him. His whole philosophical method was based on a cold, precise, mechanical view of the world which set rational thought in opposition to the 'unreliable' world of sense perceptions and which he used to try and prove the existence of God – needless to say without success.

Indeed, his perception of God could not be further from the idea of a God within all things. In his theories of physics, he, like Parmenides and the atomists of ancient Greece, denied the concept of a vacuum in stating that, if there is nothing between two bodies, they must be contiguous. In philosophical terms, this physical theory denies the existence of a void and thereby the notion of an expansive spirit, an 'empty' space, which is not subject to reason.

Descartes is the end of the line which began with the elemental division between body, mind and spirit in Ancient Greek philosophy. Every important facet of his philosophical method is in essence a means of establishing a method of dualistic thinking which remains unquestioned to this day. With his insistence on trying to prove the existence of God, he sharpens the divisions between spirit and thought. With his distrust of the world of the senses, he drives a wedge between the mental and physical worlds. With his belief in the determinism of this physical world, he blasts away the notion of free will and sets up a basis for the absolute rigidity and authority of materialism. With his 'logical' premise that one must always start from a position of doubt, he opens the way for the pessimistic scepticism of philosophers such as Hume a century later.

Such is the legacy of Cartesian philosophy, as the material, rationally comprehensible world becomes the only accepted reality – an all-encompassing reality in which even the image of God must come under its definition, thereby excluding any innate sense of a greater, spiritual Unity of infinite connections which extend far beyond the scope of our rational understanding.

Chapter 9

Materialism and Fear

From this point on, with the exception of a handful of 'mystical' philosophers such as Spinoza and Schopenhauer, philosophical inquiry points downwards towards the material world.

If one is to look at Descartes and those who followed him in a favorable light, one could certainly say that, on one level, he did look back to the ancients and reaffirm the necessity of using our personal experience, albeit devoid of our sense perceptions, as a basis for knowledge. Once one accepts that the search for the connection to the Source has been swept aside by the need to create a better material life for all, the most positive inheritance of the philosophy of Descartes' successors is the sense of individual conscience which we know as liberalism: on one level, the liberation from the tyranny of medieval power imposed from above; on a broader level, the lack of any rigid political or religious dogma.

Also, from the 18th century onwards, the momentum for change shifts from the control of the Latin world to the more open and less 'god-fearing' society of the North. The heirs of the Cartesian legacy, with its uncritical, optimistic belief that absolute knowledge is attainable by man, were the British Empiricists who, through their complete devotion to the material world, had a profound and lasting effect on the social patterns of the Western world.

England had escaped the horrors of the religious wars and was a relatively tolerant society with the power of the Church and State always to a certain extent regulated by the moderating influence of parliament and a powerful middle-class. Therefore, unlike Descartes and his followers on the Continent who existed in a world of sharp divisions and therefore felt the need to bring an all-consuming sense of order into their theories, the British philosophers took a more down-to-earth approach and dealt with the more material and practical elements of life, with particular emphasis on improving the lot of the individual.

The humanism of the Renaissance, with man in the center of the world, was brought to an extreme with these materialist philosophers. Descartes' rationalism was concerned with innate ideas and thoughts with our senses of no relevance whatsoever, thereby leaving the field open to those who saw, as Locke and his followers did, that our senses are the conduits of our experience and are therefore our only source of knowledge. This purely physical view of human knowledge is, in a sense, a culmination of the process begun by Thales and the Miletian philosophers who first proposed that the fundamental nature of the Universe was a substance. However devoid of spiritual feeling, the philosophy of Descartes tried to encompass the existence of God; the Empiricists' concern was exclusively with the material world.

On a human scale, there was certainly a positive aspect to Locke's ideas with his political theory leading to an ethic of enlightened self-interest and individual responsibility. Yet, in putting all his emphasis on man's material needs and in ignoring man's spiritual nature, the die had been cast and the way was open for his successors to take the realm of ideas further into the quagmire of materialism: Berkeley's belief that 'To be is to be perceived' finally excludes any connection with an immaterial, Universal Source, while Hume's dismissal of the rationalist's causal connection between events, replacing it with his sceptical view that they are merely a succession of sense impressions, denies that there is any integral order within the Universe itself.

Finally, with Hume, we come to the debasement of human inquiry. He denies the existence of the 'soul' or any higher self; he rejects any connection with a greater Whole; most absurd and arrogant of all, he refuses even to consider anything that is beyond the scope of our senses. Following the example of Descartes to the extreme, although abandoning the rational precision of his 'Method', Hume assumes that all must start from a position of doubt and the purpose of inquiry is to do the best we can and, failing any answers, follow the customs of society.

No wonder, therefore, that this desiccated view of the world should arouse a reaction just as extreme on the other end of the spectrum: the nebulous movement which has been termed Romanticism. In contrast to the dry and complex rationalism of the day, the 'noble savage' fulfils the ideal of an innocent simplicity which transcends a world increasingly bogged down with material values. Romanticism surges out of the need to find spiritual nourishment, but, in a world where the spiritual connection to the Source has been lost, its energy is instead focused on depth of emotional sensation, hazy ideals and the excitement of living on the edge.

In its highest form, Romanticism is a desire to return to the 'innocent' simplicity of primitive societies. However, without the Universal Authority of the Group which existed within them and without a sense of connection to the Whole, this ideal came to be manifested as more of a need to witness the destruction of the old ways in the vague hope of a better world arising out of their ashes. The romantic hero is no shaman whose individual power can heighten the awareness of the group consciousness; he is a lonely figure obsessed with his own inability to fit in with the degenerate society around him.

So it is that there came to exist the dualism of rationalism and romanticism: on the one hand, Voltaire's acerbic wit and absurdly rational optimism expressed so glibly in his Candide, and, on the other extreme, his antagonist Rousseau's self-indulgent dreaming and championing of feelings over reason. These two extremes, combined with the scepticism of Hume, helped to create an atmosphere of disillusionment in a world which was ripe for change. When this change did come, it was in the form of revolutions throughout the Western world, the intention of which was to break the grip of the existing ruling elite, but out of which there ultimately emerged only one common, enduring victor: the materialist ethic.

Although the great revolutions are often seen as the liberation of the working class, this is far from reality. Whoever it was that eventually took up the banner, the prime, motivating force behind the greatest of them was, in the initial stages, nearly always the middle-class and the material ethic which was inextricably bound up with it. In both America and France, for example, the source of revolt was first and foremost the middle-class's anger at being heavily taxed by the established ruling class.

The French Revolution has a particular place in the institutionalization of materialism and the seemingly total abandonment of spiritual idealism. While Locke's England was creating a more open, liberal society, 17th century France was being dominated by the absolutism of Louis XIV. During this century, France was the admired cultural center of Europe, imitated by petty princes throughout the Continent, and Louis XIV established a regime in which he saw himself as the heir to the longest line of succession in Europe and therefore as inheritor of the role of God-King. This illusory egotism had surfaced from time to time with certain Emperors of Rome, Charlemagne and others; with the authoritarian power of Louis XIV, we come to the final, debased flourishing of the idea of the God-King which originated as far back as Ancient Sumeria and Egypt. In this pompous, self-glorifying figure, unadulterated ego in the material world has long since replaced any sense of connection to a higher consciousness.

There is much evidence to show that the ill-fated Louis XVI and his queen felt a much more genuine sense of responsibility towards their subjects than their grandiose predecessor, but the excesses of Louis XIV's regime had created such debt that the new king had to impinge upon what the bourgeois class saw as their sacred right: their material wealth. Events had passed beyond the king's control and the method of his demise – the guillotine, a mechanical contraption severing the head and brain from the body and heart – symbolized the clinical nature of the new era which was to follow. The ideal of the monarchy, a line of hereditary God-Kings, absolute but benevolent rulers, was dead, and any attempts to revitalize the institution in later years were mere illusion. The succession of Emperors and Republics which followed the exile of Napoléon in 1815 was simply an irrevocable progression towards a new hierarchy based on material wealth which differed little from its predecessors in its determination to hold on to power at all costs.

Indeed, the revolutionary anthem of 'Liberté, Equalité, Fraternité' proved to be but an illusion. The romantic fervor which had so vehemently espoused the vague ideal of liberty now directed its energies towards the passionate and intolerant notion of nationalism, which ultimately led to new autocratic and totalitarian governments. Although Napoléon instituted throughout the territory of his conquests a civil code based on merit and individual rights of property rather than the old system of privilege, creating a temporary, genuine drive for constitutional, liberal reform, this structure was ultimately used by his successors – a new brand of nationalist, autocratic leaders, such as Bismarck and Louis Napoléon – to consolidate their own positions of power. They in turn were supported by a new merchant class and a new breed of philosophers, such as Hegel, who, looking back with fear to the disruptions of the past, felt the need to create a rational premise for an external, imposed order, bringing the individual back under the 'protective' wing of the State.

However, the supreme victory for materialism occurred in liberal England with the dawning of the Industrial Revolution, where thousands of common people who had earlier been released from serfdom now unwittingly flocked into the new urban centers and into a new kind of slavery away from any connection to the Earth which had nurtured them, however sparsely, for so long. And with this new triumph of the material ethic, there arose a new kind of benevolent, material philosophy, where any notion of a connection to a non-physical Source of All Being is of total irrelevance, given that conscience is tied to an atheistic, purely physical view of the world, where equal rights and the greatest happiness for the greatest number of people is the fundamental aim, even to the exclusion of the ideal of liberty.

In this new world, those with a heightened social conscience were of course a mere drop in the ocean of an increasingly despotic order – not the old-fashioned despotism of a hereditary ruling class, but the despotism of materialism itself, where Darwin's survival of the fittest became a literal symbol of the capitalist ethic of 'Eat or be eaten', and where the Napoleonic code of merit was replaced by the ruthless exploitation of the masses by the new quasi-feudal, self-made masters of the industrial world. Even the Civil War in America, best known for the victory of liberalism over slavery, ended the old system of privilege only to open the floodgates for the expansive, Northern, competitive, urban mentality to establish its own structure of inequality, based on wealth, which endures to this day.

The romantic ideal which had at first embraced liberalism now found its expression in nationalism – no doubt, at first, as an expression of native culture and folklore, but ultimately succumbing to the totalitarian ethic which arose within the boundaries of these new nations which had thrown off the yoke of religious control. This was particularly the case in the Northern Germanic states which were united under the ruthless discipline of Bismarck and where even art and music were increasingly drawn into the social and political arena.

As the Industrial Revolution spread from its point of origin in England to the Continent of Europe and in particular to the increasingly powerful and expansive Prussian state, the material ethic became the focus of these new nationalist blocs – and of the competition and rivalry which was a natural result of unadulterated materialism.

Possessions in their simplest form had created conflict from the very earliest civilizations; with materialism reaching a new peak with the Industrial Revolution, the same root of conflict took hold in an amplified form: Fear – the fear of losing these physical, external, transitory trappings of power which had long since blotted out the eternal light of the inner spirit.

It was this fear, the continuous, absurd shifting of alliances of the late 19th century which, in hindsight, makes the First World War seem so inevitable. It was this fear, combined with the rational ability to create weapons of mass destruction without an intuitive sense of responsibility and connection to one's fellow men, which made the resulting, gruesome carnage possible. It was the rational sense of separateness, of one race above all others, which swept Hitler to power and provided the justification for the mass, cold-blooded slaughter of another race – a dark race, serving as a focus for the latent fears hidden deep within the subconscious of the light Aryan race, the warriors of the Sun.

And, despite the memory of this horrific slaughter, geno-cide continues to this day, where perceived difference can be an excuse for mass annihilation, where the conscience of an individual or a race can be smothered by the fear of and therefore aggression towards someone of different race, culture, sexuality, class, to name but a few of the distinctions artificially created within the rational part of man's mind.

We live in a world in which this rational mind, shrouded in the cocoon of the material ethic, has subjugated our intui-tive nature which sees the eternal connection between all living things and reaches out to the infinity of the Source of our Being. Cut off from this innate sense of the Whole, our psyches are dominated by fear and by guilt, and, instead of looking forwards to a new world, our leaders are obsessed with maintaining the status quo and suppressing any threat to the existing 'order', using the simplistic absolutes of 'good' and 'evil' to enforce a rigid morality, the prime purpose of which is to quell the creative force of individual conscience.

This dualism of good and evil is at the heart of modern reli-gion which is supposedly our guide towards our higher selves, but which in reality promotes the conflict and strife which now pervades the world. I do not need to catalogue the hatred and wars throughout the world which continue under the guise of religion, supposedly setting one force of good against another force of evil. The religious hierarchies seek to prolong their pre-carious hold on power by maintaining the 'divine pendency' of their teachings, so that their subjects blindly follow a code of archaic, 'pre-ordained' precepts without understanding the distant nature of their origin and thereby their limitations and often irrelevance in our constantly changing world.

Of course, one cannot blame religious institutions alone, for this conservatism, this fear of losing what one already possesses, has infiltrated all levels of human existence, from governments down to our familial and individual lives. Lying at the heart of this conservatism is the fear of the poten-tially destructive power of the individual ever since it was unleashed from the original Universal Authority of the Group by the supremacy of the rational mind. We fear the burden of our own individual responsibility and therefore look to an externally imposed universal authority to make decisions for us. Whether we live in a totalitarian or a so-called democratic society is irrelevant, for the essence of this mentality is that we surrender our responsibility to an outside power which we can blame if things go wrong.

The rational mind, materialism and fear are strange bed-fellows. We allow ourselves to be swept along by the driving force of the rational mind which creates the diversity of our material existence, yet we do not have the courage to accept responsibility for the effects which this has on our planet. We see the continuously changing sequence of events in the world around us, but we act as if everything is immutable and set in stone. On the one hand, we follow our sequential minds to a specific end: the idea of success or failure, dreams of a new job, a new house, comparing our ambitions and achievements with others', hungering after new ways to occupy our mind; on the other hand, we cling to our habitual patterns through our fear of the unknown; we comfort ourselves with the familiarity of the material things around us; we do not question our behavior and beliefs as we are afraid of the infinite possibilities which our free will opens up to us.

All of this implies a total lack of faith in our inner being, that part of us which is connected to the Source of All Being. Because we have failed to understand the nature of our evolution into the individual, conscious beings we have now become, we still believe deep within our psyche that the self cannot be trusted. From birth, we are told what is right and what is wrong – only a few have the courage to go out into the world to learn for themselves and stand up for what they *feel* is right. Even fewer are prepared to see the illusion of the material world and to search within themselves for their own individual Truth.

If we look back over our evolution, the age of the Universal Authority of the Group was the age of innocence – innocence in the sense that we had neither the power nor the volition to actively change our own destiny and the destiny of the world around us. The ultimate destruction of this Authority by our rational forces brought us into a new era in which we gradually gained this power and, in doing so, expanded our consciousness. It has so far been an era of immense upheaval, not only within our collective and individual psyches, but also in the way that we have recently wrought havoc on the physical world around us. I believe that the main reason

132

why this upheaval continues unabated to this day is that we have refused to recognize the power of the evolutionary force behind us – we have struggled against it rather than shaping it to our benefit; we have clung too rigidly to the roots of the past, rather than trusting that we can bring into Unity the totality of our being, rational and intuitive alike, to forge a great future for our species and the planet as a whole.

The many ways we can do this, ranging from our personal lives to the more expansive concepts of government and dominion, are the focus of the second part of this book.

Part Two

Duality into Unity

Chapter 1

A Matter of Life and Death

So much for history and the analytical style which went with it. The second part of this book will be written in a much more personal style, for the changes we are all confronting at this time are of an intensely personal nature. As this section progresses, I shall move on to broader themes, such as education and government, but my primary focus will be on the ways in which we as individuals can begin to bring Unity back into the core of our beings. Only when this occurs on a personal level will the impetus for a greater planetary change take root.

It will be of no surprise to me if you, the reader, are presently going through a period of 'crisis' in your own life. This could be a major personal crisis or, even more likely, a feeling deep down within yourself that you are in a state of limbo: you know that many of the things you used to take for granted no longer have any meaningful validity in your life; you are beginning to feel that one stage of life has come to an end, yet you do not know where you are being led as your new direction.

I make this point here, as it is important for you to understand that you are not alone in this. Wherever it is that you are living, there are many people who are going through a shift in consciousness, even if this is something that they cannot articulate. There is an increasing sense of anticipation, often mingled with fear, that 'something is in the air' which is going to turn our world upside down and sweep away much of what we clung on to in the past because of its familiarity. I say anticipation mingled with fear because our true inner being knows that the time is right for such a change; our 'small' self which sees this material world as the only reality fears the loss of the blanket of material security around us.

I shall delve more deeply into the nature of the changes in the following chapter, but, first of all, I wish to focus on the one dualism which lies at the root of the mentality of fear which pervades our modern society: that of Life and Death. I do so because the way in which we face death ultimately points to whether we as individuals are capable of bringing Unity into the core of our existence. All else that follows in this book, from our personal growth to the broader perspective of the society we wish to create, comes down to this one Question: 'Do we feel and trust our connection to the Whole to the extent that we see the death of our physical form as a mere transition from one state of consciousness to another?'

Now, I do realize that it will be a rare man or woman who can in all honesty and truth answer a 100% Yes to this question. I know that I cannot – 99% maybe, but there will very occasionally creep in a glimmer of doubt in my mind, that 'unconnected' part of me which, in certain moods, still demands proof! But, then, doubt and the questioning that comes with it are inextricably tied in to the path of expansion and consciousness which we have all chosen in this human existence and without which we may just as well have been born as a rock!

Of course, I cannot persuade you with words that death is a veil which we pass through from one dimension to another. This is something that you feel or you don't, just as you either know within yourself that we are all part of a Whole – a Source of our Being beyond our understanding, or you believe that the physical world is all that exists. Or, most likely, you have a sense of the former, but you have not adjusted your thoughts and actions to reflect this feeling.

Let us look at how your attitude towards 'life and death' affects your existence. Supposing that you grow up within a conventional family and educational framework and absorb the ideas and 'morality' which your particular segment of society considers the norm. During adolescence, you rebel with the natural instinct to assert your independence; you are subject to new outside influences, as well as to that burning need to express your own individual feelings, sexuality and creativity. Often, this appears to run in opposition to the narrow focus which you have been brought up with, and the struggle between this new personal energy and the pressure to conform will probably represent the primary, inner conflict of your life to this point.

At this stage, the question of life and death is not of paramount importance, as an adolescent does not generally look forward to his or her death as being particularly real. However, from this point on, the way you perceive the 'reality' that you call life and death comes into play and determines the fundamental way in which you choose to live your life.

If you see this earthly existence as the only reality, you may go through your adolescence and even your early twenties being a bit of a rebel, trying out lots of new experiences, but always in the background of your mind is the knowledge that some day you are going to have to grow up and take on responsibilities, just as your parents did. You end up getting a job, settling down, getting married and having children, as most people do.

It is at this point that the material world stakes its claim on you. Bound within the finite notion of life and death, you accept a pre-established order for your existence. Once you have your nuclear family, you accept that the main thrust of your life is to nourish this family within a blanket of security. If you are the mother, you are the focal point of the home and you probably work too. If you are the father, your job becomes a primary focus of your life, and you consider yourself responsible for providing material prosperity which you see as a perfectly acceptable end in itself.

Once this pattern is established, it usually moves forward inexorably, as individuality loses out to the increasing need for comfort, familiarity and as few surprises as possible. You continue to go to work five days a week, your children eventually leave home and you look forward to retirement when you can hopefully relax and do all the things you never had time for. Within this framework, you very quickly make up your mind as to how you wish to live. As an adult and parent, you have your own fixed view of the world, of what is right and what is wrong. You do not see your life until your dying day as a constant source of flux, change and growth, as this would always be negating your acceptance of the pre-established limits of what one can do. Specific ambitions are all well and good, but you can't keep on changing and moving in new directions all the time. If you only have three score years and ten to live in, why not make this short span as easy and comfortable as possible? And when you see that it's coming to an end, certainly it's frightening, for you do not want to leave all this behind, your loved ones, your wonderful house and possessions; but then, we all have to go sometime and we may as well put as good a face on it as we can!

On the other hand, how would it change your life if you knew that life continued after death and that you lived in a Universe in which everything was interconnected and part of the same Whole? Everything would seem to be so much more fluid and full of possibilities, and yet so much more awe-inspiring, as it would mean that you have absolute free will to choose the course of your destiny, and the pre-established limits which you took so much for granted and which were so comforting are nothing but illusion.

And maybe the yogis are right when they say that this material world is 'maya', the world of illusion. Maybe it is just the arena in which we play out our own growth, expand our experience and awareness.

So, if you do not see death as the end, how does this change your life? If you trust in the intricate connections of the Whole, then you see your life to be in constant flux, as every thought and every action will have an effect which will ultimately return to you. As in the previous scenario, you may choose to get married, get a job and have children, but this does not alter the fact that your life is constantly changing and therefore does not fit into a nice little ordered package once you have assumed these 'responsibilities'. Instead, your responsibility is to be true to yourself and to be of service to others wherever you can. By being true to yourself, I mean always doing what you personally feel is right, rather than following the dictates of a society which has long since abandoned any pretense of condoning the free expression of the individual. By being of service to others, I do not mean this merely in terms of the narrow confines of the family, but wherever in your day to day life this service is needed.

Without question, this limitless view of life presents you with considerably more challenges and sometimes more hardship than the finite view of existence which tends towards conformity. It is so much easier to exist within set boundaries, for the choices are not so great. If you wish to remain within these boundaries, that is fine. No choice is right or wrong. Each choice is an expression of you as an individual. However, once you open yourself up to an expansive view of life in which your earthly sojourn is but a stage in a long journey – then, be prepared for the unexpected and understand that courage and strength are needed to follow the often rocky path of your own continuous growth.

So what does all this have to do with a Return to Unity?

We are both physical and spiritual beings, and the great challenge of our earthly lives is to integrate these into One. I remember reading somewhere words to the effect: 'We are not physical beings trying to be spiritual; we are spiritual beings working on the physical plane.'

Spiritual is the term I use for our eternal essence which exists far beyond the confines of our earthly existence, whereas the physical is the vehicle we have chosen to reside in for a finite period. Within this physical body we are in a sense trapped; we are presented with challenges throughout our life, and, if we do not like them, we cannot just escape from our bodies and run away. We must ultimately face them, for, even if we turn our backs on them, the same lesson will sooner or later return to us in a different form.

For me, spirituality has nothing to do with organized religion, although it can of course be found in those more open traditions which encourage the individual to discover his or her own spiritual path; nor does it have much to do with the extremes of the New Age Movement which talk about spirituality in such airy-fairy terms that I sometimes wonder whether they are living on the same planet as I am.

For me, spirituality is understanding our connection to the Whole and to our fellow beings and living our life on the principles which lie behind this understanding.

Let me be more specific about my personal interpretation of how this means I approach my existence.

My primary motivation is to search for and live the Truth, which leads to a sense of Unity with the Whole and to a feeling of inner peace and tranquillity. Like the early Greek philosophers, this quest is both hampered and enriched by my rational mind, which divides everything up and draws me away from any sense of connection with the Whole, yet which also gives me a frame of reference related to the knowledge and experience that has been handed down to me over the years. Alongside this linear intelligence is my intuition, my 'intelligence of the heart', which does not judge and separate like the rational mind, but which draws upon an innate well of knowledge connected to the natural order which lies within the Universe, the Whole. My intuition also guides me towards a realization that my Truth is mine alone and therefore cannot be forced upon another.

When I look at the major decisions I have made which have propelled me along a new direction in my life, there have been but a handful, yet they share one thing in common: none of them have been meticulously planned. They have arisen out of seemingly nowhere, and, by the time I have acted upon them, there is always a sense of inevitability about them. It has felt so right and so perfectly natural to follow these new directions that all the little voices of fear which accompany any major change were of no consequence. Also, once the decision was made, these changes were so easy and effort-less that there could be no turning back. Other directions that I have in the past tried to follow because I have felt I *ought* to have become so labored and beset with obstacles that I finally understood that it was time to turn away from them.

This is the dilemma of the choices one makes in one's life. If one persists in a finite view of life and death, then one is often guided by a sense of obligation and conformity – doing some-thing just because it feels right is considered to be selfish and irresponsible. If one understands that one's intuition is a guide to a deeper reality beyond one's rational comprehension, one can only act according to one's own conscience and beliefs, even if such an action may be considered wrong by others.

Sometimes, decisions are made more difficult because we are afraid of what others will think of us. This fear of being rejected or judged by others is as fundamental to our behavior as our fear of death, as it goes to the core of our feeling of lack of self-worth which has been instilled in us over the long years of our evolution. Fear and guilt go hand in hand with a mentality which is cut off from the Whole, the Source of Being; instead of understanding that we are beings unfolding along a path of greater awareness and consciousness, we judge what we see as our own faults and limitations, and then, of course, we will find fault in all that is around us. Instead of being proud that we have chosen to embark upon the difficult journey which we call our mortal existence, we treat ourselves with as little respect as a hard taskmaster does when he whips a lame mule.

It is a difficult concept for us to grasp that we have chosen to enter into this physical form, especially at such a time of turmoil as this. However, think back again to the Greek philosophers' attempt to define things in terms of form. If we were beings of pure spirit, unbounded, then how would we experience the opposition and strife which is the essential creative force within our evolution? There would be no Set to stimulate the growth of the divine principle of Horus.

Our physical bodies and the physical world around us are what create form within the boundless nature of the Infinite Whole, and we choose to incarnate within this form to explore new levels within our own consciousness. The fact that strife, hardship and conflict are part of this experience is due to the power of duality, the separation from Unity, as an evolutionary force. It is also a tribute to our own courage striding forwards, often blindly, but trying to make sense of it all.

But, of course, we cannot make sense of it all purely by virtue of our rational minds. On one level, our rational minds can lead us to the extreme of Good on the physical plane by our attempt to make this material world a fairer and more just place to live in, where we offer ourselves up not only for our own growth, but also in service to the needs of others who may not have as easy a life as us. There are many who do so without any strong belief in the eternity of life beyond our physical plane, who act simply out of the eloquence of their hearts. And yet, even giving comfort on the physical level to those living in deprivation can only go so far; the only way we can get to the root of social inequality and injustice, as well as other things which we see as being wrong with our world, is to start with ourselves, our own inner guidance and to work towards creating a shift in consciousness on a broader level, which is to open people's eyes to the Unity of all Creation.

There can only be Unity between men if there is an understanding of and faith in the Unity of the Whole, the Universe.

Chapter 2

Man, Earth and the Universe

The Gaia Principle – a physical view of Unity of the Earth and its components – is now widely accepted, yet an understanding of a greater Unity which far transcends the world of our sense perceptions still barely exists, even in the minds of those who are concerned about the havoc mankind is wreaking on the planet which nourishes us.

Strangely enough, it was the science of physics, that pinnacle of the rational mind, which began to unravel, in the form of quantum mechanics, many of the rigid laws which had for so long blinded the inquiring spirit to a deeper reality. More than anything, the scientific mind had been seen as proof that our rational powers were capable of not only encompassing but also explaining the world about us. Yet, at the beginning of this century, physicists began to discover that the subatomic particles they were investigating appeared to have a will of their own and invariably refused to follow patterns which the scientific mind could predict. In acknowledging this and realizing that they could no longer predict absolute truths, only probabilities, scientists came to what was at the time a momentous conclusion: that a total understanding of 'reality' is beyond the scope of our rational minds alone.

What is almost as remarkable as this discovery itself is the fact that it has made little impact beyond the world of science. It seems not in the least to have shaken the confidence we have in our intelligence, the scope of our rational powers. Our philosophy and actions are still based on the belief that the world is governed by absolute truths which exist quite independently of our own existence. We are still convinced that our minds perceive reality as a whole, as opposed to recognizing that our rational side can only assimilate individual facets of what we experience through our senses and convert them into our own, personal reality.

The nature of 'reality' is a subject which has obsessed the minds of philosophers for centuries. Let us take a vegetable, a cauliflower for example, and look at its growth in terms of our perception of reality. What we see on the surface is the edible part of the cauliflower itself. We see it grow or die or eaten by birds; what we do not see are the roots and the myriad of micro-organisms and chemical reactions within the earth which affect its growth.

The obvious reply to this is that this is an oversimplified analogy. Although we only see the cauliflower itself, we could, given the right scientific equipment, observe and deduce what is going on beneath the surface.

A modern scientist's reply to this statement would be that it is incorrect.

First of all, you cannot deduce exactly what is going on beneath the surface. You can get out your microscope and observe in greater detail the reactions taking place, but even this detail is limited. Just as you cannot see from above the surface exactly what is happening, you cannot deduce exactly what are the root causes of the reactions you are now observing. You can try and work out what is *probably* happening, but the deeper you delve, the less certain you can be.

Furthermore, there is the question of your own involvement. In classical physics, the scientist acts as an independent observer who has no relation to the object of his observation. According to modern physics, you cannot presume that your very act of observation is not changing the reaction itself. The modern scientist sees himself not as an observer, but as a participant in his experiment. In the new world of science, there is no such thing as a separate reality – we are all part of the same all-encompassing organic pattern.*

In philosophical terms, the difference between classical, Newtonian physics and quantum mechanics can be defined very simply. The former sees the Universe as being governed by laws which man, as a superior, rational being, can comprehend and define; the latter sees man as an integral part of a Universe beyond the scope of our definition.

The fact that the former has held sway for so long and continues to do so says much for the apparent need of our species to believe in an absolute power, whether a god or our own intelligence. Surely, centuries ago, Galileo's use of the telescope, his ability to observe something that the naked eye could not see, should have raised doubts about the potential of man's intelligence as opposed to elevating it to a higher plateau. Once we acknowledge the existence of phenomena that cannot be directly perceived by our own senses, we have to admit the likelihood that, however many scientific advances we make, we shall never reach the Source. In recognizing that our sensory perceptions account for only one superficial layer of the physical world, how can we presume that the number of layers beneath it is less than infinite?

Yet, the fact remains that the classical view of the world still governs our actions and behavior today. The reason why is perfectly understandable. On the surface, the new world view confronts us with a terrifying void, as it leaves us with no absolute truths to cling on to. When orthodox religion was the prime motivating force, the word of God was the word of absolute truth. He passed down his commandments and, if we followed them, our reward lay in Heaven. From the Age of Reason onwards, the need for an almighty god became smaller, as the confidence in the power of own intelligence became greater. Yet, we still followed very much the same values and absolute truths, (as well as adding new ones on the way), the only difference being that we now saw them as being products of our own rational judgment.

Absolute truths, whether of a religious or rational nature,

---

*For a more in-depth investigation of the scientific principles behind this, I recommend Gary Zukov's *The Dancing Wu Li Masters* and Fritz Capra's *The Tao of Physics*.

give comfort and security. A philosophy that denies the existence of an almighty, external God and equally rejects the supremacy of man's rational powers would at first appear to destroy this security and advocate chaos. Just as religious uncertainty was seen as a threat to the structure of society in seventeenth century Europe, a lack of faith in man's rational powers could be judged as a threat in today's society which views man as being in control of his own destiny.

In reality, the opposite is the case. Traditional morality – the clear-cut division between good and evil, black and white – has proved itself totally inadequate in dealing with the many levels of our existence and is the source of much of the conflict in today's world. It is one thing to advocate a simple behavioral guideline such as 'Thou Shalt Not Kill', which protects the sanctity of life; but when the concept of absolute truth is used to judge a complex situation, it only succeeds in creating a void between the two poles of 'right' and 'wrong', instead of trying to reconcile the myriad of disparate elements which lie in between. If one dismisses the concept of absolute value judgments, the two poles merely become different points within the same spectrum – they do not exist as separate entities.

Moreover, any judgment we make can only relate to ourselves. Since our intelligence cannot totally encompass Reality, we have to acknowledge that the reality we observe is merely our personal interpretation of Reality. These interpretations are the roots of our ideas – they cannot be based on absolute truths, as they are based on our own experiences, our limited observation of Reality. We cannot assert that these ideas are applicable to anyone but ourselves, as each individual has their own perceptions of reality, built on the accumulated experience of their own lives.

Needless to say, this view of the world makes any absolute value judgment obsolete. An inflexible, inherited system of judging human behavior merely serves to limit our understanding of each other. We proudly use the term 'objective' to demonstrate how 'fair' we are in arriving at a conclusion, yet, in fact, objectivity is an illusion. A mind that can create an objective truth does not exist; our ideas are bound by what we perceive and what we are taught.

What we perceive and what we are taught – these are

the indefinable world of impressions and the precise notion of analytical facts. Once more, we come back to these two words, the intuitive and the rational, and the apparent opposition between them: the one seeming to passively absorb the Whole, the other assimilating elements of the Whole and breaking them down into quantifiable parcels which can be related to human experience.

However, even this dualism is an illusion, as, in a world of Unity, these two aspects of our being would be complementary, the one feeding the other. At present, Western society places such emphasis on the power of the analytical mind that our intuitive perceptions are generally shunned. Our minds dart so rapidly from one specific element of our lives to another that it is no wonder that they are subject to so much stress and confusion. We are perplexed and even afraid when confronted by something which cannot be solved or explained in rational terms, as there is no deeper Source to turn to.

Within this modern mentality, where the mind sees the physical world as the only reality, there is an intrinsic fear of the void, just as most children fear the dark, or rather the unknown lurking behind it. The void, denied by philosophers from the Greek atomists to Descartes, represents all those elements of existence over which the rational mind has no control. It is the very expansiveness of the Universe, within which lie the intricate connections which our limited view of the world cannot begin to fathom.

At the very heart of the void is the phenomenon which we call 'Chance'. If we choose to accept the modern scientist's view of the world, consisting of countless subatomic particles, we can relate chance to our own physical existence and see it in terms of the random distribution of these particles which combine to make us genetically what we are. (In the most broken down form comprehensible to the scientific mind, these may be represented by DNA, but we must of course understand that DNA itself is merely a recognizable phenomenon which is in itself an accumulation of as yet unrecognizable, unpredictable phenomena.)

If we look at chance in terms of our own experience as we pass through the continuous flux of our lives, our interaction with the people and events that come our way appears, likewise, to be random, unpredictable and beyond our individual control. Such a perception of the role of chance in our lives is bound within our limited view of physical reality.

However, in a Universe, a Whole where all is interconnected within a natural state of Order, what we see as chance takes on a completely different significance. Although the events which confront us in our lives appear from our limited perspective to be random, everything which crosses our path does so for a reason, for what we see to be the unpredictability of a random, chaotic, purely physical Universe is in fact the innate balance and order of a Whole of which the physical is just one manifestation.

As I have previously stated, we are all spiritual, eternal beings living at present on a seemingly finite, physical plane. There would be no point in this existence if our consciousness were not to grow and expand from our experience of it, and, therefore, as we walk through our lives, we are constantly presented with challenges which force us to explore paths which have been hitherto unknown to us. What appear to be chance encounters or occurrences are in fact the process by which the forces of the Whole that lie beyond our understanding bring into our lives the essential lessons we must learn in order to become more complete.

This is probably the hardest shift in mentality to make for someone who has been embedded in a world which sees everything solely in rational and material terms – not only because this new interconnected reality seems beyond our rational comprehension, but also because it means that we can no longer shy away from any challenge which we encounter. It is no good blaming other people or 'chance' for what appears to go wrong in our lives; instead, we need to accept that any challenge, however difficult or painful it may appear to be, presents us with an opportunity to work through some important aspect of our being which has not been fully resolved or fulfilled.

This is the essence of Faith: not the old way of believing in an external, omnipotent God, but the more participatory expression of trusting in one's connection to a greater Whole. In the old way, people used to passively pray for God to put things right for them and blame 'cruel fate' if things went wrong; if we trust in our connection to the Whole, then prayer is a very powerful, active tool by which we may request for inner guidance as to what we ourselves can do to move through and learn from a particular challenge in our lives.

We cannot of course begin to comprehend the levels of existence beyond our physical plane of this Earth, but, in a sense, such an understanding would be of little relevance to what is the essence of our mortal lives: our personal growth. As long as we believe in the Unity of all things, we can then trust that everything which confronts us in our day-to-day lives – whether we consider it good or bad – is there to stimulate us to learn and grow more quickly, to expand our consciousness.

Of course, I can only speak from my own experience. It was my own confrontation with death which awoke me from my former very rational perspective, and it was the slow path from this crisis in my life which led me to feel this connection to the Whole which I dwell on so much. Having made the shift in consciousness, it has now been a matter of putting it all into practice. It is one thing to write and read all this theoretically in books, but it is quite another to infuse every thought and action of one's life with such a consciousness of Unity.

There are many steps in this process, but there are two in particular which make the path easier and more direct. The first, as I have already touched on, is the understanding that there is nothing which occurs in our lives without a reason. Therefore, a seeming obstacle, even something as momentous as a serious illness, is a means by which we are being prompted to take stock, delve deeply into ourselves and confront elements within ourselves which need to be worked through and resolved. I shall focus on this more in a later chapter, but I just wish to say here that life need not always be a major struggle if one can learn to see through the surface of a situation into the deeper reality behind it.

The second is the realization that Newton's third law of motion does not just apply to physics. 'To every action there is an equal and opposite reaction' applies equally to the energy we put out in our lives. If one can grasp the notion that everything we do has a consequence and that everything we put out to others will ultimately return to us in some form or other, then this brings the whole business of 'conscious living' to a new, amplified plane.

When I am talking about the energy of our actions, I am not talking about 'good' or 'bad', as these are futile terms.

The whole concept of us being punished for things we do that are bad is absurd, as the Whole of which I write is not an avenging God; it is purely a matter of balance, summed up by the law of motion quoted above.

An acceptance of this 'law' brings individual conscience to the fore. You can no longer act in a certain way just because it is considered the norm, as you cannot then put the responsibility of the consequences on an inanimate principle such as a norm. If you do something to conform to a certain standard while not personally believing in such an action, you will set in motion a cycle whereby you will ultimately in some way experience the consequences of running away from your intuition. This is not a punishment; it is simply a matter of learning and growing, which is what we are all continuously going through in this physical world.

The more we act in conflict with our intuition, our individual conscience, the more imbalance we shall attract towards us from which it will become more and more difficult for us to extricate ourselves. Sometimes, it may seem to be difficult or even hazardous to follow our own Truth, especially when it runs counter to the opinions and approval of others, but the ultimate effect of doing so is, on the ethereal plane which connects our individual actions to the Whole, to cut a shining path through all the dead weight we would otherwise allow to build up around us. At first, you may not be able to see the immediate consequence of following your own Truth; however, as you get into the habit of it, you begin to feel your connection to the Whole and to your Higher Self, so that the decisions confronting you become easier to make and your whole life takes on a lighter quality.

This leads me back, finally, to the matter of seeing the rational and intuitive as complementary in the world of Unity. The rational side of our heritage has an important role to play in our development and growth, as we cannot fail to recognize from man's evolutionary path: it pushes us forward to experience and learn from all the different facets of the huge diversity that our earthly life offers us. Yet, we have seen what occurs when this is not counterbalanced by our intuitive side – that part of us which remains in touch with the deeper reality beyond our rational understanding.

Neither one nor the other is superior, because, as I wrote in the previous chapter, we are spiritual beings living on the physical plane and our challenge in this earthly life is to integrate the one with the other, so that there need no longer be a conflict between the part of us which is driven forward to expand our experience and the part of us which desires to return to Unity. Once this balance is found, then the Unity of the Whole itself will expand.

So far, I have written about the effect of our connection to the Whole personal growth, but what is the effect of humanity's actions upon this same Whole? In a world of balance and Unity, the one cannot affect the other without there also being a reaction in the opposite direction.

In religious terms, we are brought up to think of a God from whom all emanates and from whom we must all learn. It would be considered preposterous in Western traditional religion to think in terms of God 'learning' from us mere mortals and expanding through the experience which we undergo in our day-to-day lives. But, within a Whole in which all is interconnected, how could it be otherwise?

It is not the role of this book to delve into the many forms of existence beyond our particular physical realm,* but the life form we call mankind does not of course live in a total vacuum, and the intensity of our experience and evolution, in particular during a time of extreme change, does not just affect our fellow living beings on this planet. Every vibration of change, however tiny it may appear to be at the point where it occurs, creates a ripple which spreads out to the very limits of the pond we call the Universe. Likewise, every shift in vibration which occurs on a Universal plane cannot help having an effect on our own, individual lives.

At present, the Earth, and therefore ourselves as the highest form of conscious life living upon it, has entered a new cycle of change where the finite notion of what we call 'Time' becomes compressed, so that what occurs in our lives begins to appear to take on a greater intensity. As I have shown in

---

*There are many esoteric books which do this. I recommend *Mindweld: A Cosmic Embrace* as a good starting point.

the first part of this book, such periods of seemingly sudden transformation happen on a regular basis, but we have now reached a particular point of 'crisis' where mankind as an entity is faced with a choice: whether we wish to create a renewed sense of harmony and Unity with the Earth, having already pushed our 'separateness' to the limit, or whether we will pursue this 'separate reality' which we have created to the point of divorcing ourselves completely from the energy of the Earth; or, to put it in more concrete terms, we have reached the point where the Earth will or will not continue to sustain us. The choice is ours.

Of course, as we are all eternal beings, the latter course does not mean that we shall cease to exist; it simply means that we will create for ourselves a new, denser reality, which is more in keeping with our materialistic actions and thought forms, while the Earth itself will move into the new, heightened vibration which is passing through it at this moment in time. We can deny that we are being faced with the ultimate challenge of transforming the essence of our being or we can face this energy of change in every aspect of our lives and turn in faith to the knowledge that we can move into a new reality for which our inner being is yearning.

The depletion of the ozone layer and the 'greenhouse effect' are very real physical manifestations of the knife edge upon which we sit, but they are indeed just physical manifestations. Scientists and governments argue as to their seriousness and to the steps which should be taken to counteract them, when it appears perfectly obvious that this is a warning that we can no longer afford to create a world of imbalance and disunity. It is not merely a matter of reducing damaging emissions; it is more fundamentally a matter of creating a new world of Unity and Balance on every level of our existence.

Chapter 3

The Unity of Love and the Power of the Dark Side

As I keep on repeating, it is somewhat pretentious of anyone to believe that they can change the world without first
changing themselves, so it must be at the personal level that
any fundamental transformation must begin – often easier said
than done!

The obvious question is: 'Where does one start?', and my
answer, however vague it may appear, is simply: 'Be aware!'.
In fact, there is nothing at all vague about constant awareness;
it is the basis of the day-to-day existence of any conscious
being, in that it is the means by which we subject our every
thought and action to our conscience – that part of us which
decides what *feels right to us*.

Now, at this point, it is important for me to define what I
mean by the word 'right', as the traditional, so-called 'moral'
interpretation of this word lies at the root of many of the problems which mankind has created for itself and the Earth over
the past two millennia.

As has been observed in the first part of this book, the word
'judgment' and the concepts of 'right and wrong' are closely
connected to a sense of separation from the natural state of
Unity which exists within our world. As we have evolved along
our path into the rational beings we have become, the role of
individual conscience has been increasingly suppressed and

155

absolute judgments as to what is right or wrong have gradually been etched in stone within societies ruled by rigid structures of control whose main priority has come to be the maintenance of order at all costs. The Ten Commandments are probably the best known example of such social strictures, given a divine pendency in order to make them 'morally' enforceable.

During the breakdown of internal order which existed in Old Testament times, the imposition of these external rules of order were perfectly comprehensible within the framework of an essentially nomadic tribe which was trying to settle within an established community, yet this does not mean that these same rules can encompass the complex needs of a society which has evolved and changed in every conceivable way over the two and a half thousand years that have elapsed since then. Moreover, they presuppose a distrust of the elemental power of the individual, which continues in our society to this very day.

When I write about 'what I feel is right', these words have nothing to do with so-called universal precepts, but place the emphasis back on the responsibility of the individual. Therefore, in this context, the word 'feel' presupposes that intuition is as important as the intellect in reaching a decision; the word 'right' only applies to what seems the best course of action to the individual at any given time, and has nothing to do with absolute 'moral' judgments. Basically, I am returning to the idea of internal order which rests in opposition to an externally imposed order; or, to put it another way, I am raising an inner sense of right above a handed down tradition of right.

Contrary to the fear and distrust of self which has become inherent in our modern society, this reliance on the inner sense of right is not a threat to order, but an expanded version of the Universal Authority of the Group which maintained a natural order within the early evolution of our species. However, whereas order was in the past maintained by the innate cohesiveness of the semi-nomadic group and its natural connection to the energies of the Earth, the only force that can bind together as disparate a group of individual energies as we have on our Earth today is the Unity of Love.

Love is the internal order which binds all conscious creatures together. It is the essence of the Christ Consciousness which, having been rooted on our planet by the man we call

Jesus and by many others, is now beginning to come to fruition. If that sceptical part of you sees as unrealistic the ideal of creating a world unified by Love, you are failing to understand the immense power of Love, once it becomes fixed in the hearts of enough people. Love is not a mere emotion or passion as portrayed in popular songs or romantic literature; it is a powerful energy force which has a vibration of its own – of a much higher frequency than the forces of rigid control which are still attempting to resist it.

However, the power of these forces of control should not be underestimated. The source of this power is what spiritual Masters have long since referred to as the 'dark side',* which is the energy created by the continuous process of man cutting himself off from those aspects of himself which he has judged as negative, thereby allowing them to develop into powerful entities unto themselves. The concept of sin and separation has become so established deep within the psyche of those who hold power that the means of holding on to this temporal, material power is to 'divide and rule'. It is in their interest to nurture separation through intolerance and competitiveness, for this necessarily weakens any threat to the structure of inequality upon which their survival depends.

Love is the very antithesis of this mentality, as it does not see distinction between men. The dark side will continue to insist that a world based on Love is a mere illusion, because it will always assert that man is a selfish creature and cannot be trusted without an external structure to keep him in place. Meanwhile, it will continue to create laws and prohibitions which will take the individual further away from exercising his own responsibility and make him more amenable to a life in which decisions are made for him.

Yet, what we must also understand is that, if we start to judge this seemingly immutable, controlling power which governs our society, we are missing the point, as the behavior of our governments is fundamentally a direct reflection of the way in which we behave in our own lives. Just for a moment take a look at yourself over a period of twenty-four hours and see

---

*Or, even more appropriate, the 'Shadow', without which we could have no perception of Light.

how much you separate yourself through judgment from other people and from certain of your own thoughts and actions. Even those people such as myself who see Love as the only path towards creating a better world fall into this same trap again and again. We are so deeply conditioned to behave in this way that it is difficult to get out of the habit, even though we may consciously try to do so.

In a sense, this is the crux of the matter. Sometimes, the more we strive, the harder we are upon ourselves when we fail and our own image of ourselves takes a tumble. It can be an all-consuming cycle, which drives us onwards to do better but drives us further from self-love when we do not meet our expectations of ourselves, just as we fall into the trap of judging others when they too fail to act according to our expectations.

This is something I see in myself and in most other people who are seeking to open up their spiritual path, and I believe that the strife between Horus and Set in ancient Egypt illuminates how we can work through this. In that myth, we see how Set always represents the Dark in opposition to the forces of Light, which are first embodied by Osiris and Isis, and finally by Horus. As you will recall, it is not the victory of the Light over the Dark, of Horus over Set, which ultimately breaks the cycle of conflict. It is only when Horus and Set become *reconciled* that the cycle is complete.

In many ways, Set could be equated to what is disparagingly referred to as the Ego in modern day 'New Age' language. In this language, the Ego is supposed to represent all that is bad, which runs counter to Love, in our modern world. The Ego represents all that is selfish and destructive within an individual's behavior: all that sets him apart from his fellow living creatures upon the planet.

And, yet, as we saw in the first part of this book, it is that same Ego which pushed mankind to explore to the limits of personal experience, without which man would not have evolved into the being he is now. It is ridiculous to question whether this evolution was right or wrong, as we are now what we are. To judge a certain part of our evolution is to judge what we are today; to judge what we are today is to deny the forces which have contributed to our evolution, and it is through denial that we have created the energy of the 'dark side'.

Just as with Set, the life force of the Ego is strife and opposition, and these are both creative and destructive forces. Whether they are creative or destructive is for us a matter of choice. If we see Ego as part of ourselves and work with it to learn from the experience and to expand our consciousness, then we can harness its energy and use it in a creative way; on the other hand, if we deny it by cutting it off from ourselves as being 'evil' and unworthy, then it will fly off with an energy of its own which will sooner or later rebound to us with a force which we may not so easily be able to handle.

On the most basic emotional level, an example of this is the result of suppressed anger. If we have been conditioned to believe that it is bad to express anger, then we will suppress this emotion rather than directing it at the source of the anger. Of course, this does not mean that the anger has disappeared, but rather that it builds up inside us until it explodes, often more violently than the original anger, at someone or something which bears no relation to the original source of anger.

The more extreme results of suppression and denial of emotions are what we call disease. The traditional view of such chronic diseases as cancer, AIDS etc. are that they are caused by an external agent such as a virus, yet this is only a very small part of the truth. A virus is one of the simplest life forms on this planet, and the human body is probably the most complex organism. When the human body is in a state of total balance and harmony, which doctors call homeostasis, the intricate systems within it ensure that a virus or any other invading organism is unable to have any destructive effect. However, every living human being is in varying states of imbalance due to the emotional stress of the world we live in, and the effect that an invading organism has on our physical body is very much dependent on the way in which we deal with our emotional lives. Suppression or denial of our emotions is one of the best ways in which we can create imbalance within our bodies and attract dis-ease into our being.

Working on my own health and working with chronically ill people was, in a sense, my personal training ground. My two previous books, *AIDS and the Healer Within* and *Trusting the Healer Within*, were the result of this work, which is why I choose not to delve too deeply into the question of health and disease in this particular book. However, what is most important to recognize is that disease can be the most powerful stimulus for inner growth, as opposed to the object of fear which it has become in our modern, technological society. Almost without exception, in my experience, those people who have gone into remission or cured themselves of AIDS, cancer, chronic fatigue syndrome (M.E.) etc. are those who have come to the realization that their dis-ease is a signal that there are things deep within the core of their being which need to be worked upon and released. Instead of putting their faith in their doctor to cure them by popping a pill into their mouth, they take up the challenge of finding their own inner balance – certainly not an easy task, but the rewards are worth the effort!

The health of the physical body finds its correlation in any organism – from a close family unit, to a particular community or nation. Where there is suppression or denial of any facet of our being, whether emotional, psychological, behavioral or any other means by which we express our creative energy, this cannot fail to have an effect upon the fabric of the world we live in, even as far reaching as the Earth itself, which can absorb only so much of the imbalance which we force upon it.

So, ultimately, we come back to that force which we call Ego, personified by Set, or judged in Judeo/Christian terms as Satan. What does it mean and how does our understanding of it guide us towards the realization of Love in our lives and in our society at large?

The essence of Ego is the separation from Unity which was documented in the first section of this book. On the most fundamental level, it is tied in with consciousness and awareness of self, leading on to the growth of the rational mind which divided everything up and was the impetus of our singular evolution. It has, as we have seen, been responsible for great creativity and great destruction.

On a modern, behavioral level, the separation of Ego manifests itself as competitiveness, ambition, the desire to prove oneself and seek approval of others. It is a driving force which feeds the individual's need to achieve and succeed. This is seen by many as what 'makes the world go round' and by others as what has brought this world of ours to 'the sorry state we find ourselves in'. Both could be said to be true.

However, what is most important to me is the question of what lies behind this force which drives humanity onwards to either great advances or towards self-destruction, and I believe that the answer lies back in the Creation myth of Adam and Eve, and the peculiarities of the very Western emphasis which I highlighted in the first chapter of this book.

Somewhere deep within our psyche is a profound sense of fear and guilt associated with our 'Fall from Unity' and this appears to manifest on two different planes. First of all, there is the shock of Jung's 'Psychic Birth'. Just as an infant emerges from the comfort and darkness of the womb and has its last physical connection to its mother, the umbilical cord, cut, so man emerged from the security of the Universal Authority of the Group into the bright and often lonely and frightening world of individual consciousness. Admittedly, this was spread over a longer period of time than the instant of physical birth, but, in terms of the linear ratio of man's evolution, the time scale is barely different. The result is a dichotomy deep within us as if we are still young children or adolescents: on the one hand, still clinging to our mother's apron strings and subconsciously yearning to return to dark void of Unity whence we came, and, on the other hand, exploring the light of day and pushing out-wards to the limits of our individual power.

Secondly, and more specifically Western, is the burden of guilt that somehow we have done wrong to acquire this knowl-edge and 'stray' from the Unity which nurtured us before we were born into this new, bright world. In the Garden of Eden, the serpent, Satan, the tree of knowledge, the duality of sexual-ity – all of these are seen as evil, as the temptations which have lured us away from what is 'good', yet we know that without them mankind would never have evolved and may just as well have continued to live in the trees of the forests.

Therefore, we cannot say that any of these particular aspects of human evolution are bad, as they are part of our nature; instead, where we went astray was the way in which we abused these wondrous gifts which had been offered to us. From the story of Cain the settler murdering Abel the herds-man to the ancient myths of Atlantis and Lemuria, as well as the evidence of the rise and fall of the great civilizations within our historical knowledge, the finger points again and again to the same source: mankind's inability to have dominion on this planet without abusing the power and responsibility this has entailed.

In the stories of Atlantis, Lemuria and even Noah if we take away the artificial creation of an external God, the common theme is a race which is given all the wonderful gifts of the Earth, where all is plenty and in perfect harmony. We are also given the great gift of free will, where we choose how to exercise the dominion and responsibility of maintaining this harmony, while at the same time exploring new avenues of consciousness. In all of these ancient stories, there is a wonderful Golden Age, where Unity exists alongside consciousness, but ultimately this Unity fades, as man begins to use these gifts and knowledge for his own ends, choosing to ignore his original, innate understanding that all is to be shared between all living creatures. Soon, even the sanctity of life and the sacredness of the Earth is forgotten, so that man no longer appreciates the gifts offered to him nor seeks to maintain the natural balance and harmony which he inherited. This continues over a period of time until men raise themselves up above other men and forget that the blessings of their physical existence were gifts granted to them, but rather see everything emanating from their own knowledge which they feel free to use as they see fit, irrespective of the consequences.

Finally, as a result of this straying from Unity, there comes a specific moment in time when the natural balance has been disrupted to such a degree that the greater harmony of the Whole needs to be restored and the source of imbalance must be swept away, either by flood, earthquake or whatever other means the Earth has of re-establishing its own equilibrium.

The rise and fall of the great civilizations such as ancient Sumeria, Egypt, Greece, Rome, let alone more recent ones, are a microcosm of this process, differing only in that they are superseded by other civilizations or by periods of turmoil, as opposed to being totally wiped out. The root cause, though, is the same: the abuse of power, the inability to use the plenty and diversity of the world for the benefit of the Whole – in other words, separation triumphing over Unity. And, today, we have reached not only a pivotal era, when it is a matter of choice as to whether our current civilization survives; we have reached, through the immense technology we have created, one of those definitive periods when we can choose whether man-kind survives as it is and strides forward as a force of Unity, or whether we too will be swept away by a force which will restore the necessary balance and harmony, irrespective of our desires and of our fate.

The knife edge upon which we sit hinges on the opposing forces of Guilt and Love. We have a powerful, inbuilt guilt and fear of our individual and collective power, which is reinforced by every judgment we make of ourselves and those around us. Many of us also have a deep yearning for a society built on Love, which we know represents the ultimate evolution into a Unity within the sphere of conscious life.

At this point in time, the guilt and the lack of self-love which comes with it seem to hold sway. Deep within us is rooted the knowledge of the horrendous consequences of the abuse of power which I have just discussed – if one believes in rein-carnation, this can be seen as the weight of these actions perpetrated by us as individuals and carried through from many lifetimes; if one does not, it is the accumulation of the experience of mankind's abuse of power passed on from gen-eration to generation.

If we relate this primeval guilt to Ego, one can well see the considerable effect it has on the way we behave in today's world. All the facets of behavior which relate to the Ego, such as driving ambition, the need to prove oneself or to be loved or approved of by others, show a deep insecurity and, more to the point, a strong lack of self-love.

Self-love is a state of inner peace and stillness, in the knowl-edge that every thought and action is an expression of self and therefore not a cause for blame. If we feel remorse for having done something, this is a safety valve to teach us that this is something we can learn from and not do again, where our own conscience sets the limits of our actions. This is quite distinct from guilt, whereby we judge ourselves and see such an action as negative, thereby disassociating ourselves from it.

The immense power and energy that guilt and the resulting denial generate can never be underestimated in our modern world, for it feeds our sense of separation and denies our divine nature.

On the personal level, one of the most destructive results of guilt and denial is addiction. Whether this takes the form of alcohol, drugs, sex, eating, spending money or a whole range of compulsive behavior, the truth is that no addiction just arises of its own accord. It usually begins as a means of escaping an inner emptiness or an outer unpleasant reality.

Guilt is the best way to perpetuate such a condition. The more we judge ourselves for behaving in an addictive manner and the harder we are on ourselves for each 'lapse', the more our self-esteem will slip and the more addictive the pattern will become. This is the way guilt works, for it puts energy into the object of its fury and, in doing so, gives it power over us, binding us even closer to our addictive behavior.

Where there is an inherent lack of self-love to begin with, this force becomes even stronger, especially when one buys into a judgment by society as to what is right or wrong. In a world where our individual conscience often takes us far away from what the rigid strictures of society deem to be acceptable, the stress of following our own truth can be immense, and many are so burdened by the guilt of not conforming to the socially acceptable norm that, after a brief adolescent fling, they find it easier to fall into line, rather than risk the disapproval of their peers.

This is why the dark side of human nature has flourished for so long: because few have the courage to stand up for what they truly believe in. It is a process which has become so ingrained through generations of control and surrender of responsibility that few people are even aware of the extent to which denial rules their lives and ultimately suffocates the light of Love which is their natural heritage.

On an energetic level, the result of denial is quite simple, as explained earlier on in relation to health and disease. But, denial has an even broader effect in that it is the very antithesis of self-love. If one denies or judges any particular emotion or action, one is fundamentally separating oneself from it. As we know, the essence of Love is Unity, and this means embracing and taking responsibility for every thought, emotion or action which emanates from us. If there is some emotional blockage or some persistent behavior which we see as being detrimental to our being, then self-love is the process whereby we nurture this imbalance within us and try to integrate it into our being, rather than pushing it away and judging it as something which should be rejected. The separation of 'sin' has created monsters in our world.

The inability to break this pattern of denial and absence of self-love is the reason why there is so much abuse in our modern world. Judgment and an inherent feeling of lack of self-worth are passed from generation to generation with increasing power, in particular by parents who have themselves been abused as children. Where there is absence of self-love in the parents, this will be passed on to the child, even in seemingly innocuous remarks. Where a parent's inner self is unfulfilled due to the fact that its expression has been denied by the stronger need to conform and thereby seek love and approval from others, then this need for fulfillment is often transferred to the child. When the child does not meet these expectations, which, in reality, have nothing to do with the child's own inner self, then judgment comes into play once again, and the child takes on board a sense of failure which transfers into a lack of self-love and self-acceptance.

Needless to say, the cycle continues when the child becomes a parent. It is a cycle which must be broken in this generation if we are to turn our world around and create an atmosphere of Love on this planet.

How do we begin to do this? It must always start with the self. We may think that we see what is 'wrong' in other people, and can certainly give advice if it comes from the heart rather than a point of judgment, but each individual is ultimately responsible for him or herself. The greatest change you can perform is to work on yourself, to be constantly aware of the way in which you judge yourself – and what you judge in others, as this is often a reflection of what you judge most deeply in yourself.

'Love thy neighbor as thyself', Christ said. Therefore, if you do not love yourself, you cannot love your neighbor!

The key to reaching that state of self-love is to accept that your every thought and action is an expression of your being. If you are uncomfortable with any of these, the answer is not to judge or deny them; the essence of healing is to reconcile them into your being, see what they teach you about your needs and about any feeling of lack you have within you.

Being constantly aware and delving into the depth of your

being is by no means easy, so be gentle with yourself. Learn to forgive yourself and others.

It may sometimes appear that, as soon as one thing is resolved, something else even more powerful may come up and you wonder when it will ever end. Be patient and trust your own divine nature. Once you set out on your own inner, spiritual path away from separation and guilt towards Unity and Love, there is no turning back, even though the challenges may be great.

Also, beware of superficial answers. There are many people around today who come out with such platitudes as: 'If you only learn to love yourself, life will be full of roses.' Whereas there is truth within this statement, it also implies that you do not need to get your hands dirty. There are many people who are floating in the air and do not recognize that you have to go deep into your emotions, your sexuality, your issues of power and control and integrate them into your being with acceptance and understanding before the light of self-love can shine through. Anyone who tells you otherwise is into their own trip of denial.

As this light of self-love shines from the core of your being more and more strongly, the love that you are capable of feeling for others increases accordingly. As you peel away the layers around you that consist of other people's emotional baggage and you allow the core of your being to express itself in its own individual, creative way, then the need to judge yourself and others falls away, and Love becomes a state of being.

Love is a state of being, not an emotion.

Love has little to do with the 'falling in love' of romantic songs, as this has more to do with expectation and projection than the inner stillness of Love as a state of being. Nor does it have anything to do with relating to people on a superficial level. You may be with someone as long as you like. You may talk to them, sleep with them, have sex with them, but, unless you really open your heart to them and in the process allow yourself to be vulnerable, this has little to do with Love.

When you open your heart, the energy you release is like a blazing arrow that cuts through all that is superfluous and all the layers of protection that people build around themselves. The state of loving means going directly to the core of people, seeing them clearly as they are without judgment.

Love is neutral. In its highest form, it is perfect balance and Unity, which is why it is the ultimate healer.

It is also the balance of giving and receiving. If you constantly put out 'love' and are unable to receive it, this has more to do with the need than Love.

Love is also the ability to feel compassion for those who are suffering and in pain, and most difficult of all, it sometimes involves the understanding that, however close a person may be to you, you must ultimately allow them to make their own choices.

There are many levels of Love. It all starts with self-love. Then there is personal love. Finally, as Christ showed, there is Universal Love, seeing the divine Light in all living beings, even those who appear to be shrouded in darkness.

In its highest form, Love is the greatest expression of our relationship with the Whole of which we are all an integral part. It is the inner desire to express Unity in every aspect of our being and to live in peace and harmony with everything and everyone around us.

At this time, many of us feel the need to recreate a world based on the Unity of Love, but we are discouraged by what we see around us. This is where Love as the active projection of Self comes into play.

First of all, though, we must understand and come to terms with the power that lies behind the 'dark side' which we see being manifested on every level of human existence at this present time.

The conflict, intolerance and hatred which is evident throughout the world at this moment is a direct result of the process of separation which has gathered momentum from the time that man became a creature of consciousness. As I have shown in the first part of this book, this went hand in hand with our evolution into the dominant species on this planet, and therefore to judge this process of separation as evil is as absurd as the Roman Catholic church creating the notion of original sin.

Man's rational powers have been responsible for the great material and technological advances we have made, yet the cost of this has been the resulting fundamental divisions which have arisen between one human being and another. The most extreme modern example of this process was the extermination of the Jews by the Nazis.

The starting point of this horrendous act was the clear separation or feeling of superiority of the Germans over the Jews, coupled with the resentment that the latter had control over much of the former's material wealth. However, the most powerful forces of all were those which caused the leap from a mere awareness of separation to the need to destroy: pure intellect combined with fear.

Pure intellect, the dependence on the rational, divisive side of man to the exclusion of his connective, intuitive nature, is the very essence of the 'dark side', and could not have been more evident than in the methodical, ordered way that the extermination was planned and enacted, almost as if it were a clinical, scientific experiment.

However, this process would never have reached its culmination if this sense of separation had not been fed by fear: the deep, subconscious fear that the mysterious dark race aroused within the great, white 'Master Race' which saw itself as the symbol of Purity and Light striding forth to spread these values with a blazing sword over the world.

Throughout history, this white, male, rational force within man has feared and therefore suppressed within itself anything which represented its seeming opposite: starting in early times with the male feeling threatened by the mysterious reproductive powers of the female and her connection to the cycles of the Earth and the Moon; moving through the Greek ideal of the 'arete' of the warrior and the glorification of the rational subconscious; leading towards religions of control which denied the personal, inner spiritual path and the elemental power of human sexuality; culminating in the acts of attempted genocide which continue to this day.

The Holocaust was a warning to humanity of the consequences of creating a world devoid of Unity, yet, however abhorrent this act may seem to us, we have still not learned the lesson that it was merely a reflection of the separation which existed within the heart of Western man at that time – and we delude ourselves if we believe that our present day society is appreciably more tolerant than the society which existed just fifty years ago.

At the apex of our society is a governing class whose

primary interests are to conserve and consolidate its own position of power. Its means of doing so is the age-old, proven method of creating a greater sense of separation between the different groups it supposedly governs. So obsessed are these men with the material world and the control they wield that they truly believe in the truth and rightness of this world of material illusion, inequality and separation which they have created. The only force which drives them now is the fear of losing the power they have.

They do not understand that such power is built on illusion, and that the 'dark side' of separation is an energy which has grown through being cut off from the fundamental life force of humanity. Yet, they are beginning to recognize that their power is crumbling, and like a cornered rat, they are not likely to allow it to die without a struggle.

This is why the active projection of the self through Love is the only way in which we can create change around us. The greatest temptation and the best way to increase the power of the dark side is to judge it and in particular those 'leaders' who thrive on creating separation. When Christ said 'Love thine enemies', he understood the power of men's thoughts and words. He knew that the dark side thrives on hate and fear. We may at times feel anger, in which case that can be channeled into action, but, in the end, the strongest force is Love.

Now, of course, it is quite possible that all this talk of the power of Love may seem very airy-fairy and unrealistic to you, but this is because you have not understood the true extent of the energy of change which is sweeping through this planet at this time.

History evolves in cycles and we have seen that changes occur at a much faster rate at specific periods of mankind's evolution. We have entered such a time when the vibrational quality of the Earth as a whole is going through a fundamental shift, causing old structures built on illusion to fall and a new order to arise – the seemingly sudden collapse of Eastern European totalitarian rule took place because such rigidity and control could no longer withstand such an energy of change.

Just as the last two thousand years, the so-called Piscean Age, were very much to do with exploring the limits of personal power, so this New Age, for want of a better word, signifies a shift towards a different level where this power is to be integrated with the unifying force of Love. No such major transformation can occur without a great deal of turmoil, as the old reluctantly gives way to the new, yet, ultimately, the ease or difficulty with which we make this transition in our own lives lies in our own hands.

Chapter 4

Sex and Sexuality

Sex and sexuality are without doubt the least understood and most often misinterpreted aspects of human consciousness – and, because of our inability to comprehend their true essence, they have become divorced from the core of our being, from which ensues the absurd confusion and guilt which so often go hand in hand with the notion of sex in our Western society.

I wish to make quite clear at the beginning of this chapter that sex as an expression of Love – and I am not merely talking about the narrow idea of monogamous love which our culture seems to value so highly – is one of the highest forms of Unity which can be achieved upon this earthly plane of ours, for it is an act of conscious union between two life forces.

To understand the depth of this, we must get over the ridiculous notion that sex is merely a means of procreation. When we were still bound within our animal nature, procreation was no doubt the fundamental driving force of sexual union, with the female becoming sexually receptive only at certain specific times and the sexual act being a somewhat peremptory affair.

However, believe it or not, we are no longer bound within this animal nature. We are now creatures of consciousness who have the ability to choose when and how we have sex. We are physical beings, we are emotional beings, we are mental beings, we are spiritual beings, and sex is an expression of all of these aspects of our being. If we deny that sex has anything to do with the expansion of consciousness by imposing limits upon the expression of our sexual nature, we are judging and therefore cutting ourselves off from an essential part of our human condition. If we learn to trust the elemental powers which our sexual energy represents, we are eventually able to grasp the immense part it has to play in our personal growth: as a guide towards finding balance on the very highest plane between every aspect of our being.

In the first part of this book, we have seen how sex has been perceived as an elemental energy within each individual which cannot readily be controlled and therefore represents a threat to the order of the group or of society. In former civilizations, as in many so-called primitive societies today, this energy was brought into balance with the community through ancient puberty rites. In more modern times, the control has become more psychological, and repression of boundless sexual energy has been imposed in 'moral' terms, most blatantly by the principal Western religions through their division of body, mind and spirit.

In my experience, the most powerful spiritual teachers I have met of my own generation, whether male or female, are all people who have had a tremendously powerful sexual drive. They are people who have not suppressed this drive but have been aware of its power on many different levels, and have used it, quite subconsciously at first, to delve deeply into the hidden emotional, mental and spiritual realms of their being. These have often been people, who, in their younger years, underwent an emotional roller-coaster ride, but whose natural inclination to explore any experience opened up a wealth of inner knowledge which could not otherwise have been attained.

For our sexual energy is also our life force, or what is referred to in the East as 'kundalini' – that Earth energy which enters into our body at the base of our spine, working up through the various levels of our being, or 'chakras', until it rises out of our physical form through the crown of the head and unites with the Universal energy above. If we choose to see sex as a purely physical act meant for procreation, or if we keep our attention focused on genital contact, as many men, as opposed to women, often do, then we are limiting the creative aspect of this elemental energy and preventing it from stimulating the growth and expansion of the higher aspects of the self. In general, women have a better handle than men on associating sex with emotion and love, but to see it solely in those terms is still imposing limitation. The way we perceive and even fantasize about sex has also much to teach us about many unresolved and subconscious parts of us, particularly surrounding issues of power, self-worth and, of course, not forgetting the blending of the 'male' and the 'female' within ourselves as individual entities.

Sex is spirituality. If you believe that you can set out on the spiritual path in this age without confronting and experiencing your sexual nature, you are very much mistaken. There may have been a time when it was suitable for monks or nuns to go into a monastery and deny their sexual nature in order to focus more clearly on other aspects of their being, but that time is over. This is the coming Age of Unity, and one can therefore not deny or ignore any aspect of one's being.

Sex is an expression of the passion of life – not the mere wild passion that one associates with a 'hot' sexual experience, but the passionate expression of individual freedom and energy which has been granted to us in this physical form. This passion is the unfettered enthusiasm which drives us forwards to act, create and do the things which we feel strongly from the core of our beings. It is taking the gift of free will and living life fully, taking it by the scruff of the neck, exploring new territory and not caring one iota about what other people think. It is an expression of the joy of life which comes from the heart and which is not bound by 'oughts' and 'shoulds' and other means of control which have been passed down over the centuries.

It is no wonder that those hierarchies of authority soon saw that sexual energy was something to be suppressed because they clearly understood that the physical side of free sexual expression was just part of the story. They knew that this powerful energy was all to do with the power and freedom of the individual to break down boundaries and to explore the depth of consciousness, and they knew that this was the very greatest threat to their own externally imposed power and control.

We therefore now find ourselves in the situation where all but a few people have assumed the 'morality' which is based on the fear of this elemental energy. It has become completely ingrained in our Western mentality that sex is something which 'should' be performed within pre-established limits, to the extent that it is a rare person who will even begin to understand the true power of our sexual nature.

We all know that the Sixties witnessed a dramatic breaking down of these boundaries, but, even then, this spontaneous burst of freedom was confined to a group who were judged as 'hippies' and who were not allowed to be a permanent threat to the mainstream, where the veneer of marriage and monogamy still had to be maintained. For the conforming majority, it was still alright for a man to have his 'bit on the side', as long as he kept it quiet, whereas a woman who exhibited a powerful sexual energy would be judged as a 'nymphomaniac' as if expression of sexual energy was the right of men alone.

Over the past few millennia, male sexual dominance has mirrored the psychological and social male dominance within our society, to the extent that, however strong the feminist movement may be, woman has not to this day been able to express the true power of her sexual energy. Feminism has more to do with civil and social rights than the elemental power of female sexuality, almost as if women are afraid that the release and acknowledgment of this raw Goddess energy would recreate such primeval fear within the male psyche that men would once again find a way to suppress it along with all that has been gained for women over the past few decades. However, the time for the true spiritual power of woman to be unleashed is fast approaching – a time for woman to assert herself in much more vital ways than just in the workplace.

As we have seen, the male world has been the world of the rational mind – a mind that sees matters of the body and sex as base compared with its own shining brilliance. An understanding of the sacred nature of sex has been destroyed by this separation, by this assumption that sex is an expression of the lower part of man's nature. And, needless to say, the most powerful moving force behind this separation has been orthodox religion which has ruthlessly persecuted and suppressed anything which runs counter to what it dictates to be sacred – or, to put it another way, anything that is a threat to its own position of power and control.

This denial of the sacred and spiritual nature of sex has

had devastating consequences for both the human psyche and the human body. In divorcing the sexual act from consciousness and spirituality, the 'Christian' Church and other related structures of power have been responsible for giving it an energy of its own which has often, in the case of abuse or even less obvious forms of sexual manipulation, allied itself to the 'dark side' of human nature. In imposing a feeling of guilt on all expression of sexuality outside the absurd limits it has handed down, Western religion has itself committed the 'cardinal sin': the separation of the physical from the spiritual.

As I have said before, we are spiritual beings living on the physical plane, and denying the existence of spirit in the most fundamental expression of our physical form is in essence a denial of spirit as a whole. For this violation of Unity alone, the Churches which arrogantly presume to be the 'protectors' of our spiritual lives, whether they are Christian, Judaic or Islamic, are destined to fall. There is no place for them in a world of Unity.

It is therefore no wonder that there is so much self judgment and confusion surrounding the expression of our sexual nature. Promiscuity, rather than being the evil it is judged to be, is most often the result of a powerful need to attain a state of intimacy. Sex and intimacy are inseparably bound to each other, for they are each manifestations of the desire to find Unity with another individual. Where intimacy is not experienced in a sexual relationship, then this desire for Unity is not fully satisfied, leading on to an increased inner need to search for it again. If this inner need is not recognized and, in particular, if there is a strong feeling of guilt surrounding the resulting urge for a sexual connection, then the emptiness and lack of self-love arising from this heightens the addictive nature of the search.

In many individuals, I have seen how promiscuity has ultimately led to a deeper spiritual realization, because the extremes of this search have often led to the breaking down of old behavioral barriers and the gnawing feeling of emptiness will often lead a person to explore within the core of his or her own being for a deeper, more fulfilling reality. However, I must of course warn that there is a thin and dangerous dividing line between the exploration of consciousness through sexuality and the self-abuse and the opening up of oneself to destructive energies that can be the result of this search.

Because we see sex so much in physical terms, we do not fully understand the extent to which we exchange energies with our partner on other levels. At the point of orgasm in particular, we open ourselves up completely to our partner, with all the ramifications that this entails. If the exchange is one of intimacy which comes from the heart, (and this is not of course exclusively the realm of a monogamous relationship), then this is the fusion of two life forces which has a healing quality on every level. If, on the other hand, there are other things going on between you and your partner, such as control issues, anger or any other emotion which may have little to do with your partner as an individual, then you will be taking on board whatever is being projected on to you and vice-versa. This is why certain sexual experiences can be more draining than uplifting, and can have a damaging effect on the health of the body as a whole. This does not mean that such exchanges are 'bad'; it is merely one of the simple laws of Unity that one will utlimately receive back what one puts out.

What I am trying to illustrate is that sexual energy is a powerful force which needs to be treated with respect, and therefore a state of awareness and consciousness always needs to be present within any sexual relationship, whether it has been going on for twenty years or is a one night stand. Sex can be a great learning tool, yet, like any powerful force, it can also be extremely destructive.

The most important lesson of all, though, is to seek out and release every shadow of guilt about sex which lurks within you, for, unless you do so, sex can never be a true expression of Love. What is more, feeling such guilt towards this elemental force within you means that you are blocking it and thereby allowing it to be a disruptive rather than a creative energy within your physical, emotional and mental bodies.

Do you really believe that venereal diseases and AIDS are merely the result of a simple virus? As I explained in the previous chapter, disease has its root in a much more fundamental imbalance than the intrusion of a mere virus, and the virulence of sexually transmitted diseases, in particular AIDS, is inextricably linked to the guilt and fear which we project on to the creative life force which our sexual energy represents.

It is no coincidence that this modern 'plague' of AIDS has taken such a toll on the homosexual population of the West, as homosexuality has long been the greatest focus of judgment and therefore of the ensuing guilt that society has imposed on the free expression of our sexual nature. This judgment has taken separation to the extreme of raising one form of sexual expression above another, and again this is where the power of the Church raises its ugly head, condemning as unnatural something which does not fit into its ordered little view of procreative sex.

What is not fully realized is the extent to which homosexuality represented a genuine threat to the authority and control of the Church. In many of the pagan religions which Christianity tried to stamp out, homosexuality was far from condemned, but rather seen as a sign of someone who existed slightly beyond the normal bounds of the group and therefore often had a greater ability to communicate with the spirit world. This of course runs counter to any idea of centralized control within a religious, hierarchical structure.

To this day, many shamans are homosexual and probably the best book to document the sacred importance of homosexuals in a modern non-Judeo/Christian culture is Walter Williams' *The Spirit and The Flesh*, which illustrates the respected role which the so-called 'berdaches' had until very recently in Native American tribes. Not only are these homosexual men often a focal point for much of the sacred ritual that takes place within the tribal group, but they are also greatly trusted and sought after for personal advice.

The people who show most bigotry towards gay men and women are those who have the most repressive attitude towards sex in general. The extent of intolerance, persecution and hatred that has been directed towards homosexuals for centuries, originating with the three great organized religions of the world, Judaism, Christianity and Islam, is extraordinary since it is difficult to document any ill effect that homosexuality has had upon society. Judgmental phrases such as 'moral degradation' and 'filthy habits' have no meaning whatsoever and seem to represent yet another aspect of the typical human reaction of fear of the unknown.

Unfortunately, however meaningless these words may be in substance, they cannot fail to have a powerful effect on gay people today, whether or not they choose to 'come out'. Even those who are the most liberated and 'proud' of their sexuality cannot help bearing within them some trace of the years of abuse which have filtered through generations of intolerance. The public perception of AIDS as a 'gay disease' and the Church's pronouncement of it as 'God's punishment' increase the impact of this separateness.

In my experience, the deep-rooted lack of self-love that many gay people bear within them because of the pressure of this abuse, especially if this is not fully recognized and dealt with by the individual, has played a major role in creating the imbalance within the body which enables the AIDS virus to gain hold. And yet, on the other end of the spectrum, despite the huge physical suffering which this disease has brought about, AIDS has also been one of the greatest raisers of consciousness in the past decade.

There are many who have carried this virus around with them for years without any adverse symptoms and they have seen AIDS as a challenge which has forced them to delve deep in to their inner being, not only to create health and balance within their bodies, but also to propel them on an individual spiritual path which they may not otherwise have followed. Along this path, one of the greatest discoveries has been self-love and an understanding and acceptance of the sacredness of sexual expression in their lives. Many have understood the limitations of modern, alopathic medicine and have found their own creativity as healers, so that they have in turn been able to offer their services to others.

Homosexuality is of course not merely to do with a person finding another person of the same gender physically attractive; if it was, we might therefore just as well say that all sex is purely a physical urge and has nothing to do with our emotions and our desire for Unity. How society has managed to make this distinction between homosexual and heterosexual sex completely beats me!

There is no doubt that, in our modern, intolerant society, homosexuality is a difficult burden to bear, at least until one comes to terms with it and accepts it as a natural expression of self. However, to my mind, once this acceptance has been achieved, there are two very distinct advantages which make the path towards spiritual Unity a much more natural and obvious path for gay men and women to follow.

Firstly, if you grow up knowing that something you feel within the core of your being is right, when society says it is wrong, then this makes you naturally sceptical of all that society judges as being right or wrong. If you really trust your feeling, it gives you a head start in setting out on the path of following your own intuition, living according to your own conscience rather than conforming to the dictates of society.

Secondly, a gay man or woman has the greater impetus to reject the sexual stereotypes which have been assumed by nearly all modern civilizations and to explore both the male and female aspects of his or her nature. It is this capability which has no doubt been responsible for investing so many homosexuals with a great spiritual power in both ancient and modern times, as this balancing of the male and female is one of the great steps towards finding Unity in one's being.

Indeed, as an extension of this, I believe that, as the consciousness of mankind returns to a greater sense of Unity, man and woman will become more androgynous and bisexual, as was supposedly the case in earlier, 'mythological' civilizations. This suggestion may draw fire from heterosexuals and homosexuals alike, but, if sex is an expression of intimacy, why should this intimacy be confined to one gender? Again, it all comes down to whether we perceive sex as an expression of our highest selves, or whether we see it as something merely physical which is subject to 'moral' strictures and taboos.

So far in this chapter, I have dwelt on the elemental energy of sexual expression, but I now wish to focus on the dualism of male and female and discuss how this fits in with the projection of the image of Unity into our lives.

Whenever I talk or write about the masculine and feminine energy, I am always reminded of a discussion I had with three women friends recently in a train in Hungary. I was talking about the need to integrate the male and the female together when one of them interrupted with the words: 'This whole male/female division. It is such a ridiculous male concept that one can be put in this little package and the other in a completely separate one. In many of the old civilizations the Earth was seen both as the Mother and the Father, as was the

Sun. This is a typically male distinction.' The other two women agreed, and, of course, they were right!

But, then, I am a male, as was Jung, whose definitions of 'animus' and 'anima' took this distinction beyond sexual roles and to a deeper inner level within every human being.

Because of my friends' reactions, I am a little reluctant to write too much about this aspect of duality, as I recognize that my fundamentally rational way of describing it brings complexity where my friends' viewpoint was perfectly simple; and yet I feel bound to pursue it because I recognize that this difference of approach between myself and my women friends reflects the fundamental division which has occurred between men and women.

If we go back to the beginning of the book, we see that, for a multitude of reasons, the female energy represents a more holistic approach to the world, as exemplified by the statement of my friend. With her regular monthly cycles, woman is perceived as being more closely connected to the Earth and the Moon, while man sees himself as symbolized by the shining light of the Sun. Woman is rooted in the present reality, while man is obsessed with grand ideas of the future. Woman, in her stillness, perceives the Whole and feels the cyclical nature of life, while man divides everything up and drives forward towards a finite end. Such a list could go on for ever.

The essence of this distinction is between the expansive and the contractive. On the one hand, we have the all-encompassing Egyptian female symbol of Maat, 'the arch personification of the power of Space, Time and Matter, within whose bound all beings arise and die.' On the other hand, we have the Greek, male concept of form which creates things out of this boundless energy, so that they are comprehensible to the human mind.

However, contrary to Aristotle's belief that form is superior to matter through his regrettable analogy of the male impregnating the female, the expansive and the contractive are equal in a world of Unity. The interplay of Matter and Form, is at the heart of creativity in our earthly, physical world.

In order for this balance between the expansive and contractive to be recreated, it is now time for women to reclaim their power. This does not mean trying to compete and achieve in a male dominated world, nor has it anything to do with rejecting all that our male dominated society stands for. What is important is for women to re-establish a connection with their innate, creative force which resonates with the elemental cycles of our planet and the Universe.

It is time to reaffirm the ancient traditions of Woman in her threefold nature, as depicted in the story of Merlin in Chapter 7. There, Ganieda represents the purity of non-sensual love and unchanging, gentle wisdom, which is the basis of any return to Unity. Guendolina embodies the polarity of sexual energy and fertility in the principle of sensual love and motherhood in all its glory – not the sterile motherhood which in modern times we have come to associate with looking after the home while the husband is away at work, but in an expansive role of acting as a binding force within the community at large and with the Earth itself. Finally, there is the mysterious archetypal figure of the shape-changer with power over life and death, breaking down the old and transforming it into the new. It is she who points towards the esoteric powers of Woman which have remained hidden so long: the ability to work with the elemental energies of the Earth to create change on different levels, from physical and spiritual healing to the reharmonization of Earth and mankind.

In exploring their creativity, women can finally begin to re-assume their share of the mantle of leadership in our world, not in the guise of a Mrs. Thatcher who is a man in women's clothing, but bringing to the world their connective essence which has been denigrated for so long.

Likewise, it is time for men to surrender their absolute control over leadership and also to surrender to the 'Wild Man' within themselves, expressing their own elemental energies rather than perpetuating the desiccated society we live in, so devoid of feeling and true spontaneous action. Deep down, most men feel a frustration at having to conform to the male stereotype with a rigidity which suppresses their own innermost desires. Like Merlin himself, man must confront the duality of the material world before attaining a state of spiritual peace and Unity, but he can only do so if he lets go of the mask of control and opens up to the totality of his being: the physical, the emotional and the spiritual, as well as the mental – combining the male archetypes of the poet and the spirtual warrior within himself.

Finally, though, as man explores every corner of his maleness and woman delves down into the depth of her femininity, the true path to Unity will ultimately lead to man integrating the feminine into his nature and vice versa, for these two seemingly opposite extremes are essentially part of the same reality.

There is no room for sexual stereotypes in a world of Unity; nor can we afford to waste our energy in judging aspects of the male or female within ourselves or other people. The male/female duality still remains a powerful creative force within our world, and in order to nullify the destructive elements of resentment and judgment which we have allowed to surround this duality over generations, we need to delight in the diversity of every aspect of both the male and female nature within all of us.

Likewise, we need to delight in our physical bodies as the 'Temple of the Spirit', and, in doing so, bring into Unity the trinity of body, mind and spirit which has been sundered for so long.

Chapter 5

Relationships, Parents and Children

The most important guide as to how we have established Unity within ourselves is the way in which we relate to other people. Relationships are the essence of our lives on this earthly plane; if we did not relate to other people, we might as well live in a total vacuum. Without the wonderful and often trying diversity of our relationships, the stimulus for inner growth would be limited.

When we think of the word 'relationship', this immediately brings to many people's minds the question of partnership. From adolescence onwards, when the tie to one's parents becomes looser, the impetus to bond with another being becomes stronger, going through many stages until this is fulfilled on a certain level or, on rare occasions, until the stage is reached when the need to bond with one individual becomes less significant.

Whatever level we have reached on this path, the way we perceive this 'partnership' has a great deal to do with the way in which we relate to our fellow beings as a whole, as this intimate arena of bonding is a focused microcosm within the broader arena of our life as a whole.

This innate drive to bond with another person is the most powerful expression of Unity which most people feel within their day-to-day existence. This urge to find Unity with another person has understandably increased in intensity within the psyche of mankind as our material world has become further and further separated from the Source of our Being. Although our connection to the Source may have faded, this does not mean that our need to experience Unity has died. It must, instead, be expressed on whatever plane our consciousness is attuned to, and, for most people, this is within the realm of human relationships.

For most people, therefore, the melding together of two individual energies through Love on *every* level is the arena in which the most intense emotions are experienced – the joy and the pain caused by this desire to bond are fundamental to the human condition and to our growth as individuals.

The way in which we relate to our partners is a reflection of the way in which we relate to ourselves and humanity as a whole. It is also a guide as to how well we understand what Love truly is.

In our adolescence and quite often far beyond, our primary experience of Love is the notion of 'falling in love', which has more to do with the projection of an ideal on to the 'object of love' than with Love itself. The image we project may often be a reflection of the way we like to see ourselves or, conversely, of what we deep down feel we lack within ourselves – in either case, we are relating to the image rather than the person with whom we are supposedly in love.

Any such relationship is ultimately based upon false expectation, and once this image is seen to be illusory and the expectation is shattered, then judgment sets in. The person holding on to the image will feel cheated, although it is actually this person who has cheated himself or herself. This whole process has more to do with control and need than with Love.

Love in its highest sense is built on Unity, Balance and Trust. Possessiveness is the antithesis of this state of inner stillness. Whether you are possessive of a partner, a child or a friend, you are holding on to them because you are afraid of losing them. If two people are going to be together in a relationship, this will be so because they both freely choose to be together – if one person tries to control and smother another, the natural flow between them is destroyed and the relationship will ultimately die. Control is the very opposite of trust, and no relationship can survive without trust.

Honesty is an extension of trust. Honesty is feeling safe enough to express your innermost feelings and needs without shame or fear of offending. In relationships, as in every sphere of life, to be honest in order to confront an issue sometimes requires courage, rather than turning away from it, allowing it to create a momentum of its own.

In a balanced relationship, two partners acknowledge each other's rights as individuals and, most important of all, understand that both are ultimately responsible for their own happiness and well-being. Such mutual respect naturally enhances the sharing quality of a relationship, as it creates no sense of limitation and the individual strength of each partner feeds the other.

If, on the other hand, a relationship is built on an image or a need, then it will work on exactly the level of the projection. So often, I have seen a relationship where one person leaves his or her partner for another person and the one left behind wallows in self-pity as the injured party. But, do not let yourselves be fooled by this; if the energy goes out of a relationship, it is because the connection exists no longer or perhaps never has existed deep down between the core of two individuals. If you are honest with yourself, your intuition will always tell you the state of a relationship at any time; so many people intuitively feel a change within a relationship, but are afraid to confront it until it is too late. For we all change, and if you are open with your partner and share these changes, they do not have to lead you apart.

Again, this brings me back to the question of Surrender. If we truly have faith in our connection to the Source, we know that every relationship in our life has something to teach us. Therefore, all we can do is live in the present and allow a relationship to unfold at its own pace rather than always trying to force it into the narrow confines of what we think a relationship 'ought' to be. There are no rules and regulations as to what partnership really means; it is up to two individuals to consciously explore the depth of their connection and to set their own boundaries.

In this context, we must understand that the institution of marriage has been passed down to us from a time when it was seen as necessary for the maintenance of social order. It is not difficult to see from the Christian vow of the wife 'obeying' the husband that woman was once perceived as a mere possession of man within this arrangement – indeed, with arranged marriages which existed in earlier times, the material aspect of marriage far outweighed the idea of a sacred union between two individuals. Even in today's society, where marriage is supposedly a union based upon love, its increasingly frequent dissolution is invariably dominated by matters of money – and, of course, children.

I am sure that there are many arguments as to why the present, legal form of marriage should be maintained. I dismiss all which relate to material arrangements, as they have nothing to do with the quality of the relationship between two people. If two people choose to enter into a relationship, they do so of their own free will. If this is a relationship built on trust and honesty, there will always be communication and sharing, but, even within this special bond, there will also be an understanding that each partner is ultimately responsible for his or her own life.

Within a relationship, the only commitment one can make is in the present. To commit to spend the rest of one's life with another person is to deny the forces of change which continuously affect one's existence and over which one often has no control. The ridiculous parade to the divorce lawyer in our Western society and the even sadder spectacle of seeing two people stoically living a miserable life together both point to the absurdity of institutionalizing such 'permanent' commitment in a world of constant change and flux.

The only argument in favor of marriage even worth considering concerns the welfare of children, but I believe that this argument is yet another way of copping out of individual responsibility. Indeed, I believe that many unwanted and unloved babies are not only born out of wedlock, but are also a result of the pressure of a society which 'obliges' young married couples to procreate before they are fully prepared for the responsibilities of parenthood. This whole ethic, in particular in the Third World where bearing many children is still seen as an insurance for one's old age, has greatly contributed to the immense over-population we have in our modern world.

When I look at the young couples who get married and have children before they have had any chance to experience life, let alone to understand what Love really means, I am saddened at how the sacred union of two people has been abused by the hierarchies of power in order to keep the mass of humanity within the narrow confines of a routine existence. The cycle of childhood, school, marriage, children, a job and the illusion this gives of responsibility is in reality a cycle of control which denies the individual the freedom and true responsibility of exploring his or her own path.

As I keep on repeating, we are beings of consciousness, and creating a new life is one of the supreme acts of consciousness. Nowadays, many couples are waiting longer before they have children – partly, of course, because of the importance of career for both sexes, but also because of a recognition that a relationship needs to be built on a solid foundation of experience and mutual exploration before the commitment of parenthood is taken on.

The reason I am so much against marriage in its present, binding form is not on behalf of those who do allow a relationship to blossom gradually, but on the behalf of the masses who rush headlong into it, as if it were some end to be achieved in itself.

Why is it that we distrust ourselves so much that we feel we cannot establish a relationship and a family outside this legal and 'moral' framework? What is the basis of the social stigma of having a baby outside of wedlock or having another relationship when one is married? It is all to do with that externally imposed order which we have allowed to smother our lives over the past millennia. It is our inherent lack of faith in our ability to make the 'right' choices without 'moral' guidelines. Fundamentally, it is our inability to take responsibility not only for our own lives, but also for creating an environment of trust and honesty where people can live in harmony together.

Now, in these last two chapters, I have in a sense played Devil's Advocate as far as sex and marriage are concerned in order to show that conventional morality is forcing upon humanity a code of behavior which runs counter to individual freedom and responsibility. In fact, I am not dismissing monogamy, heterosexuality or marriage, but am merely pointing out that there are viable alternatives which are not 'morally wrong'.

The decision as to how one enters into a relationship with another person, sexual or otherwise, rests with the individual alone, and is not subject to the approval of other people. Within this decision is an acceptance of the individual responsibility to act according to one's conscience and with constant awareness, openness and honesty. In a world of Unity, if one chooses to get married, this is a personal choice which creates no strictures, but blesses the union with one's partner for as long as it lasts by means of whatever sacred ritual may be meaningful to both parties. If children are to be born from this union, then this too is an act of conscious creation.

In a world of Unity, the creation of new life and the relationship between parent and child is necessarily perceived in a much more profound manner than if one sees the birth of a child in terms which relate only to our physical lives.

In a sense, the various stages of development in a child mirror stages of development in humanity. Just as mankind in its early stages of evolution had not developed a consciousness of separateness, so a baby originally sees the world as a blurred reality in which everything merges together. Its five senses are not yet as distinct and refined as in later life, and there is still a connection with the wholeness of the Source which is lost as the child grows older. (In my own life, this link to another reality was illustrated by my three very real, 'imaginary' friends called Mockey, Vinegar and Louise Fishwater, with whom I apparently spoke at an early age, but of whom I had never been consciously aware when my parents told me about them some years later!)

A child is not just born as an instant mini human being. The spirit of the new being does not enter into the physical foetus in the womb until the contract is fully made on a deep, subconscious level between the parent and the new child. Sometimes, in the case of abortion and even miscarriage, the parent is not ready for the child to be born, or, in some cases, a lesson has to be learned by the parent through the abortion or miscarriage process. At this point, the new being who is to incarnate as the child has not fully entered into the physical body of the child and therefore neither abortion nor miscarriage necessarily means the destruction of a life in the most complete sense.

In a world of duality, of separateness from the Source, the extent of the connection between parent and child cannot be fully appreciated, for our rational minds can only see the birth of a child as the creation of a new life rather than as a new cycle in an existing being's continuing evolution. In reality, just as the parents hopefully *consciously* choose to have a child, so, too does the child make a decision to incarnate in the physical plane as part of its own continuing evolution. What is more, the child also chooses to be born into the environment which is best suited as a stimulus for its own level of growth and expansion of consciousness, and its parents are the most important ingredient within this environment.

For many people who have still not come to terms with the idea that there is an underlying order and unity which lies behind the apparent chance and chaos of our physical world, the idea of a child choosing its parents is a little hard to swallow. However, when you consider that the interaction between parent and child is one of the most creative, primeval forces in our world, does it not appear likely that, in a world of Unity, this is a relationship which is established on a much deeper level than our mere rational minds can comprehend?

Just for a moment reflect on your relationship with your own parents. Without question, parents are generally the strongest formative influence on our lives. Their influence remains with us long after we have left home and even after they have died. In our early childhood, we accept everything we hear from them; then, gradually, we grow to question until we reach that stage of rebellion where we must assert our own sense of independence if this is not granted to us. Some children are blessed with a loving, open relationship with their parents as they grow older; others become completely alienated; the majority of us find ourselves somewhere in between with much to be resolved on various levels.

Those who have had more than their fair share of conflict with their parents are often those who have carved their own path in their lives. When we come into opposition with our parents on some fundamental issue or over a whole sequence of events, we are brought face to face with the reality of calling into question those symbols and values which our parents represent for us. This in turn brings us to the point of re-evaluating all our own thoughts and actions, so that we are forced to rely on our own conscience and heart to guide us, rather than accept the ideology which has been passed down to us.

There is no doubt that such conflict causes pain on all sides, especially if this continues unabated without there seeming to be any point where the two sides will meet in the middle. And yet, in undergoing the intensity of this experience, the consciousness of the child is stimulated towards a greater pace of growth than would have occurred within the framework of a more harmonious relationship.

If you have had a life of such conflict within your family, just for a moment look within yourself and see how this has given you an extra dimension, a deeper insight into your own true essence, as well as a greater understanding of and compassion for the plight of others.

And when you see this, bless and forgive your parents, for they too have gone through their pain. While your pain has led you to a deeper perception of yourself and of others, their pain, as parents, has led them to, and may still be leading them to, the ultimate lesson of letting go of control, of learning to see their children as they are, rather than as an extension of themselves.

Children can be very unforgiving, because we take so personally everything that our parents lay upon us without stopping to think that they too had parents and probably went through similar conflicts themselves. Indeed, if we are unable to forgive and let go of any hurt that our parents have laid upon us, the resentment is liable to well up unresolved inside us to such a degree that we will find ourselves subconsciously repeating the same patterns with our own children. This is why the cycle of abuse in families continues from generation to generation and can only be broken once the emotional trauma which goes with it is confronted in a direct, honest and often painful way.

I hope and believe that a greater sense of unity between parent and child is now being ushered in by a new generation of parents who understand the necessity of creating a more balanced relationship with their children. Some would say that the modern lack of discipline within the home is responsible for the deterioration of order within schools and in young people's behavior in general, but they miss the point. What ultimately matters is the quality of the time and the communication one has with one's child.

Before the age of seven, the child is still tied very much to the mother's or nurturing parent's apron strings – indeed, in etheric terms, there is a very real cord which binds mother and child together. This bond is very important because a child, during this period, is working on a level where it still has a foot in the non-physical world from where it has come. The bond with the nurturing parents is the grounding cord in a physical sense which counteracts all the energy that is being poured into the child from the spiritual plane. This energy is fundamentally a transfer of the individual essence of the new child from the higher vibration of the spiritual plane to the denser vibration of the physical plane. If this was transferred all in one go at the birth of the child, it would literally blast the physical body apart.

This is why the first seven years of a child's life are so important. A child, from the moment it is born and even earlier, is a sentient being who picks up on every vibration around it. Although it may not at an early age have the rational capacity to understand the meaning of words, it reacts to and absorbs their tonality, so the atmosphere in the home and the relationship with its parents and between the two parents themselves will become imprinted in its psyche long before it can verbally communicate.

When one considers this, the argument to stay together in an unhappy marriage 'because of the kids' is worthless and even damaging. If there is hostility within a relationship, this will be completely absorbed by the child and will have a more damaging effect than being brought up by a single, caring parent. Indeed, the more disharmony there is within a household at this age, the more this imbalance will be reflected within the child's psyche. Where there is a lack of a grounding connection with a nurturing parent, a child will often grow up unable to develop many of the fundamental life skills which are necessary to deal with the complexity of our physical existence.* Children of alcoholics are an obvious example of those who do not have this physical grounding as they grow up.

---

*For those wishing to measure their own life skills, I recommend *The Next Step: A Life Skills Workbook for Adult Survivors of Emotional Abuse.* by Jill Raiguel.

This is why the responsibility of having a child should never be underestimated. Those who choose to have a child without a basis of love (i.e. a couple who think that having a child will help resolve problems within a marriage) play a dangerous game, the consequences of which will ultimately, in the continuous cycle of life, return to them.

One of the most positive images which comes back to me again and again when I think of the relationship between parents and children comes from a television documentary I once saw about village life in the Himlayas. The narrator remarked that the one thing that constantly struck him when filming in a particular village was the fact that he never heard a baby cry. The mother would walk around always carrying her baby in a pouch and, when she went to work in the fields, she would put her baby at the edge of the field with the other young children who would look after each other. Within this simple routine, bringing up a child was inseparable from the matter of fact business of day to day living.

In our so-called civilized society, we have lost this simplicity and, because of this, there is often a great deal of guilt associated with bringing up children, especially where mothers go out to work. It is incomprehensible to me how our male-dominated society has not established it as a matter of fact that all workplaces should have within them creches where working mothers leave their children under an employee's supervision and can spend time with them during their breaks – or even better, where mothers take it in turns to look after the children as an inclusive part of their employment.

Ultimately, though, bringing up children is all to do with love – not the bribery of showering them with an abundance of gifts and material possessions, but the warm, physical affection which is part of the nature of both women and men. It is also the understanding that the expression of love from the parent to the child is not just a one way street, for children carry within them a transformative power which is not always apparent within the parents and others who come into close contact with them.

And when they begin to explore and become self-aware, then they teach us many lessons, not least of all the lesson of trust and surrender: of guiding them along the path of what we feel is right and safe for them, but, in the end, recognizing that they must learn their own lessons and explore their own path. Only by permitting our children to have their space, by letting go of control and allowing the nature of the relationship between parent and child to change as the child grows older – only in such a fluid and nurturing environment will Love survive and blossom.

Chapter 6

Education

When we looked back on the early evolution of mankind, we saw how the expansion of consciousness and awareness within the average man and woman was tied in with the move towards greater diversity within larger settlements and the increased interaction between different races as nomadic people came into contact with sedentary communities.

The evolution of a child into a conscious being very much reflects mankind's emergence from the Universal Authority of the Group into the dualistic world of individual experience. If a child was sequestered solely with his* parents during his formative years, he would unquestioningly follow the behavioral patterns and instructions passed on by them. What makes a child into an individual aware of his own identity is the diversity of experience he has through his contact with other people.

By the time a child reaches the age of seven, he has become more aware of himself as a separate individual in his own right, who is less tied to the apron strings of his nurturing parents. It is also the age at which most children are able to formulate such abstract questions as 'What would happen if . . .?' – evidence

---

*Excuse the use of his rather than his/her which would be somewhat cumbersome!

that the rational mind has begun to assert itself outside of the well of the unconscious which dominates the psyche of a child in his infancy.

At this stage, the child has been influenced primarily by his parents and immediate environment, just as early man had been restrained within the Universal Authority of the Group. But, from this point on, this open book is susceptible to a whole host of influences from all sides. If the first seven years form the period when a child intuitively receives imprints on his character from his environment, the subsequent years form the period when his rational faculties are tuned and directed in specific ways over which he has little control.

I have made this analogy between the growth of consciousness in a child and early man, as this stepping from the blurred world of intuitive perception into the clear light of rational awareness is a crisis point for both. We have seen from human evolution that, without maintaining a sense of Unity, mankind has brought itself to another even more crucial state of crisis; if we are to give our children the chance to reverse this process, we must re-establish within them a conscious awareness of Unity, rather than denying the intuitive connection to the Whole and relying totally upon the divisions of the rational mind.

This is the great challenge of Education.

In our modern Western world, the whole impetus of education has been dominated by the need to understand and master the Universe we live in. This has also been the predominant, driving force within Western man as a whole ever since rational inquiry was brought to an elevated plateau in Ancient Greece. The whole concept of progress is seen in increasingly material terms, and education follows its lead. What is missing in both is the underlying principle of Unity.

It is interesting to note that, in Middle English, the word 'progress' signified a 'journey', more specifically a seasonal journey. The way in which our idea of progress has now been confined within the limited sphere of material comfort and technology illustrates how the inner and outer journey of man have been sundered apart and the fluid stream of our evolution has been dammed up within a limited view of our reality and our potential. The way we educate our children reinforces this stagnation.

The ancient puberty rites which exist to this day in 'primitive' societies came into being for one reason: to refocus the elemental energies of the individual child towards the good of the group as a whole. In a world of Unity, this is the primary focus of education before all else. While a child should always be encouraged to develop his own creativity and follow his own inner path, there needs to be instilled deep within his being a sense of Unity and Love which overrides all else. This is what is missing in the education of our young people.

Obviously, all such feelings must begin at home, but, however much love is integral to home life, this can be negated within a school system and by outside influences which focus on competition rather than cooperation, personal achievement rather than group communication.

This sense of Unity needs to be present not only in the obvious realm of nursery and primary schools, but right through the school system. Running alongside this is the acknowledgment of both inner and outer knowledge: the inner, intuitive knowledge connected to the well of universal consciousness and the outer knowledge of handed-down facts and rational thought.

Let me be more specific.

During the first few years of school up to the age of seven, the primary focus of an education of Unity is to instill a sense of cooperation within the child, whilst at the same time giving as much free rein within this framework to the expression of his innate creativity. Part of this process is to encourage groups of children to undertake a variety of simple projects which can only be completed by the cooperation of the group as a whole – something which tests the boundaries and the specific talents of the individual children and which will of course result in certain individuals crossing over these boundaries and learning the reactions this provokes. Creating an innate sense of cooperation in this way does not happen instantly which is why it needs to be an evolving process over a period of time within the educational structure. (This is also why the profession of teacher at all levels needs to be given new respect. Today, the status of teachers has been devalued, as they work within a degenerate educational system which neither permits them to express their own creativity nor recognizes the great responsibility they bear.)

The creative aspect of the child is to be given free rein in art, music and oral tradition of storytelling, with reading, writing and arithmetic being gradually introduced alongside them. Art and music are to be continued throughout the school curriculum, rather than being considered superfluous to 'gainful employment'. The reason for this is that they are integral to maintaining the intuitive/rational balance within the mind of the older child, as he or she is subjected to a diet of more and more individual bits of information.

In the first part of this book, I emphasized this intuitive/rational balance within the great masters of the Renaissance such as Michelangelo and Leonardo da Vinci, and even the greatest scientists of today are those who bring to their methodical research a touch of intuition or inspiration. If we are to create a new generation of inventors and innovators, we shall not do so by only feeding them with a continuous spew of individual facts. Our potential can only be fully realized when our rational compulsion to divide things up into comprehensible parts is counterbalanced by our intuitive nature which allows our mind to absorb more passively from the consciousness of the Whole. Expression of our artistic and musical creativity keeps this channel open and clear.

As an extension of this, the study of music in Pythagorean terms is an excellent means of bringing into Unity the holistic and rational aspects of Mathematics. An understanding of the harmony of music and mathematics can, at an early age, combine rational inquiry on a fundamental level with an intuitive knowledge of the natural order and unity of the Universe.

The third ingredient in primary education — oral storytelling — pertains principally to Myth. Traditional educators would no doubt consider that the power of myth would be lost on children, as it would be too complicated to explain the nuances to them, but this is of course totally false, as mythology arose out of traditions which were no more bound by rational education than six year old children are today. Indeed, a child's relatively unbroken intuitive connection to the Whole is probably more suited to gleaning knowledge from myth than the adult mind which needs to find 'meaning' in everything!

I remember, in my own childhood, discovering books on mythology at an early age and finding them infinitely more entertaining than most of the junk I was given to read by adults. If one is going to read aloud to children at school, myth is not only both entertaining and educational, but it is also of a universal quality which binds together different cultures from all over the world. In our increasingly racially integrated society, this is an excellent means of creating an acceptance of different cultures, races and colors at an early age, allowing children to see similarities within apparent differences.

Even more than this, though, it is a basic grounding in spiritual traditions devoid of religious dogma. In schools today, either there is no reference to spirituality, or what teaching there is tends towards the orthodox view which allows little room for personal interpretation.

By being exposed to myth at an early age, in particular to the native traditions of their own country – many of which have remained hidden for a long time – children are introduced to a unified notion of spiritual life in which man, woman, the earth and God are one. The fundamental beliefs and teachings of Native Americans and Australian Aboriginals, for example, are steeped in these traditions and the humor and delightful symbolism of their mythical stories are a delight to children. In Western Europe, this oral tradition has been stamped out over the centuries by the Christian Church, so we must go back to the ancient traditions which have been handed down from a time when their importance was appreciated. (In Britain and Ireland alone, there is an abundance of mythology which was spoken and read fairly universally until the late Middle Ages.)

Just as with art and music, an appreciation of myth is something to be nurtured right through the educational process as a counterbalance to the more specific elements within a 'rational' education.

Needless to say, as children grow older, they pass through the basics of reading, writing and arithmetic and their minds are led to tackle more complex subjects which make a greater demand on the sequential, rational mind. This has been the basis of education for millennia, and, as long as an intuitive, connective balance is maintained, such exploration of and building upon handed-down knowledge will remain a positive force in our evolution. Where we have gone particularly astray in recent years has been the drift towards an education the major purpose of which is to prepare an adolescent for employment – summed up most succinctly in the British Green Party Manifesto:

> The Green Party believes that the mistake has been to limit the concept of education. For too long it has meant 'training for a job'. Our lives cannot be chopped into three neat portions – learning, working and retirement. We want to provide tools and opportunities so that people can choose how to use their lives in a useful and satisfying way, whatever that happens to be. Learning is a lifelong process, and undertaken at any age and at any level it should explore and fulfil the potential of the learner.
>
> Education should cater for our creative, physical and spiritual needs, as well as the intellectual. It should encourage us to think independently, to work cooperatively, and to contribute positively and creatively to our communities. Responsible citizenship and techniques of peaceful conflict resolution are important aspects of learning. We need the basic skills of literacy and numeracy, but we also need very practical life and manual skills, environmental education, and a real understanding of the global situation.

What these two paragraphs point to is the fundamental need to completely rethink our attitude towards education, which, in modern times, has become a very rigid system the main purpose of which is to prepare us for a life within very narrow and confining parameters. Not only does it fail to take into account the intuitive, connective nature of our species, but it also seems to be drifting further and further away from the ability to train the rational mind in a way that encourages the individual to think for himself.

As far as I am concerned, the rational mind is worthless if it cannot be taught to think for itself rather than learn individual facts and pieces of information parrot fashion. This is why the whole notion of examinations is absurd, and they primarily reward those who have a good memory rather than those who can formulate and express original ideas.

The one aspect of ancient Greek education which has been abandoned in our modern age is Dialectics: training of the rational mind to define things through logical argument. If man's rational abilities are to be harnessed for the good of the world, their starting point must be a clarity which leads the individual to find his or her personal truth. (This is not to be confused with the Sophists' Rhetoric which was an intellectual game geared more towards winning an argument than searching for the truth.)

Aside from fine-tuning a young person's rational powers, this discipline of dialectics also exposes the student to conflict in a way that is not personal and emotional, but creative. It introduces the principle of strife as a creative force, as espoused by Heraclitus and Empedocles, and teaches a student to accept and appreciate the validity of the differences which exist between his and another's perception of truth without taking the implicit criticism personally. This is essentially teaching the unifying force of Love in a predominantly rational setting.

This does not mean that the investigation of the personal and emotional side of conflict should not also play an important part in the educational process. Plato, who espoused the use of dialectics so strongly, equally strongly scorned the emotional nature of man and, by dismissing this integral part of our being, he did himself and his followers a great disservice, as this led to it being completely ignored in the subsequent educational systems which are our heritage.

Human emotions and frailty constitute a very vital part of our evolution and history, and therefore cannot be ignored in education or in any other structure which man creates. We are fortunate that literature is a great chronicler of the emotional lives of men and women, and literature as a school subject has always potentially been a wonderful means of melding language and social history together, as well as involving the pupil in his or her own emotional reactions. Great literature teachers not only have to appreciate language, but must also be able to relate to their pupils on an emotional level. The teaching of literature has become very bland in our modern times. It is time to put the soul back into it.

History is also a chronicle of mankind's emotional journey. So often, history in schools is a jumble of facts and figures or a distorted, nationalist view of conflict. I personally remember spending a whole term being taught nothing but Wellington's campaign in the Iberian Peninsula. What did that really contribute to my general education?

The essence of history, as I have hopefully made clear in my own, very subjective view of it in the first part of this book, is to learn lessons from it and to understand that there is rarely pure black and white, right and wrong, in any historical situation. History is the unfurling of our evolution and is therefore inseparable from myth, which draws out of it the universal lessons applicable to all men. It therefore needs to be taught in a way which relates individual events to the world and mentality of their time, rather than in the vacuum these events are usually taught today.

In addition to this more holistic view of history, it is important for children to be able to experience history in terms of the microcosm of the region in which they are living, so that they may focus on the way in which their own communities and culture have developed from the simplest of beginnings. They should be encouraged to use their own imagination in reconstructing what it may have been like to live in earlier times – a process which not only brings history to life, but also teaches the subjectivity of historical interpretation.

This combination of the broad perspective of the macrocosm with the more personal experience of the microcosm is an important element of education as a whole, in that it teaches the adolescent mind that a particular action in a particular place often has an effect on or correlation with something occurring on the other side of the world. In contemporary education, the focus of most subjects is so narrow and utilitarian that many children leave school without having any real knowledge of the world into which they are about to enter.

This correlation between the individual and the Whole is no more evident than in matters of ecology, which will gradually take over from the more traditional geography taught in schools. The essence of ecology is understanding the balance and harmony which exists within the natural world and recognizing how mankind has seriously disrupted this balance. Unless future generations are taught this fundamental truth, as well as the collective responsibility of our race to restore this balance, there is no future for them on this planet.

This is inextricably tied-in with the teaching of science and technology as a creative rather than destructive force. It is important that all students have a grounding in science in order to understand the technology which has increasingly become part of our existence, yet the teaching of these subjects must go hand in hand with an understanding of the interdependence of all living creatures and the Earth itself. Without an innate acceptance of this interdependence, mankind has already demonstrated the destructive potential of its technological advances – something which can only be reversed once we are ready to assume the sense of responsibility to the Whole which the gift of scientific and technological knowledge demands.

These are very basic shifts in emphasis which can easily be made within any existing educational system and the starting point of this very simple approach is that students need to feel an innate connection with their fellow beings and with the planet as a whole before the rational mind is given free rein to explore and expand.

Throughout all stages of education, therefore, this connective essence of the student is to be kept in harmony with the basic rational learning process – and this is not only confined to the classroom. This cooperative mentality needs also to be nurtured within society at large, which can be achieved by including as part of all school curricula practical work in the immediate community which assists the elderly, the handicapped and others who are less able to cope with the rigors of day-to-day life. Alongside this, wherever possible, children should be encouraged to form a connection to the Earth by working on the land for periods of time.

This whole emphasis on the cooperative side of education acts as a counterbalance to the present educational system which relies too much on the rational mind's ability to break down, analyze and absorb specific facts – in other words, emphasizing the outer knowledge of passed down information to the exclusion of the inner knowledge which binds us all together. In a world of Unity, a student is only ready to proceed with the more complex and advanced aspects of education once he or she has developed an innate understanding of the Unity of all life.

This is particularly important during this 'Age of Technology and Information', acclaimed by those who see it as a new era of knowledge which will enhance the material quality of our lives, and feared by others who foresee the manipulation of this information and the invasion of privacy by the minority who holds the reins of power.

Without an acceptance of Unity, the scenario projected for the future by many of those in the vanguard of technological advances is one which will consolidate the power of the rational mind. As computers increasingly find their way into schools and homes and become linked to a global network of information, our minds will be bombarded from an early age by a super-abundance of individual facts which will take us even further from the more passive perceptions of the Whole which make up our intuitive nature. By not questioning whether we actually need a continuous increase in information and technology, let alone judging the effect it will have on the quality of our inner lives, we as individuals may once more find ourselves shying away from responsibility by blindly following the 'ideal of progress'.

At this moment in time, the direction of our education and the use of our technology rest in the hands of those who govern us. In this modern era, politics is all about money – every election is basically fought on the issue of which political party will give us more money in our pockets, and, in accepting this narrow focus, we surrender our power over the many other deeper issues which affect our lives, including education and the use of technology. If we wish to reclaim that power, we must fundamentally change our own understanding of what government really stands for, and we must learn to accept more responsibility for the decisions which affect our lives.

Chapter 7

Government

I find it most enlightening to note the connotations which the word Anarchy has assumed over the years. Ask most people what their definition of an anarchist is and the most common reply will be such words as 'terrorist' or 'revolutionary', all used in the most derogatory sense, implying individuals whose prime aim is to reduce the world to a state of chaos.

Anarchy comes from the Greek word Anarkhos, meaning, quite simply, 'without ruler or government'. In a world of Unity, where human existence is built on cooperation and sharing, could this not be considered as an ideal state, where a structure of government does not exist because it is not needed? Ideal, maybe, but not practical, your answer will probably be.

Indeed, the very thought of instantly returning to a state of anarchy would of course be one of self-deluding idealism. Human society has developed into such a complex organism that any sudden attempt to dismantle its structure would certainly bring chaos, but this is not the point. The essence of creating unity out of duality in a social sense is to work gradually towards creating a new society based on the principles of sharing and cooperation – to say this is impractical is to turn away from our responsibility as a race.

What we need to acknowledge is that, in the natural world,

life is built on a fragile balance of co-existence and mutual dependence within which there is no externally imposed
order. Such a concept of order is created by man, and government is merely an artificial means of creating a semblance
of order out of the infinite variety of our human condition.

As we saw in the first part of this book, externally imposed
government only came into being once the Universal Authority of the Group had faded. As man became aware of self, as
population and possessions grew, as inequality became more
apparent, the potentially disruptive aspects of duality needed
to be harnessed for the good of the new settled communities.
Therefore, government is a natural part of our evolution.

What we have failed to understand is that, being an integral
part of our evolution, it is an extension of ourselves. In denying
this, we have allowed government to become a lumbering
machine out of control by voluntarily ceding our power as
individuals to it. The old Soviet bureaucracy was perhaps the
extreme example of this because of its remoteness from the
people it purported to govern; yet, in democratic countries, we
fool ourselves if we believe that the superficial renewal through
occasional elections keeps government under our control.

Each successive government perpetuates the myth that it is
leading its people along a path of greater prosperity and that
each change of policy will have a major bearing upon our lives
– a mentality which arrogantly presupposes that there is a clear
destiny for mankind understandable to man, a sequence of
events which government can control. In reality, our so-called
democracies have nothing to do with government by the people for the people; their one major achievement has merely
been to fulfil the original purpose of government: to maintain a
certain degree of order, however artificial and fragile this may
be.

In those early days, the concept of order, and therefore
government itself, covered the basic need of channeling
man's energy and instincts into behavior which benefited
rather than threatened the stability of the community. Nowadays, government's sphere of influence spreads into most
aspects of our lives. It has overstepped its original purpose:
in attempting to maintain a social order, a moral order, an
economic order etc., it succeeds only in imposing a rigid set
of absolute laws which are quite unable to take into account

the myriad of disparate elements which make up our modern society.

Modern 'democracy' is a complete illusion. The fact that we exercise our so-called right to cast our vote every few years has absolutely nothing to do with democracy in the real sense. In between, we withdraw from the process of government; we may grumble and complain, but we do not participate. In the words of Pericles, we are worthless citizens.

We must not delude ourselves into thinking that we are any better than the government that rules us, as the government of a country is a reflection of the inhabitants of the country itself. This is not only the case in countries where we elect our officials, but also in those ruled by dictatorships, for dictators can only come to power if there is a vacuum left by the apathy of the people, by their refusal to take responsibility for their own government.

In the West, we are subject to a very specific form of dictatorship: the power of money and material obsession. As we have strayed further and further from Unity, the only reality we have come to accept is the material world, and we therefore put all of our creative energy into the expansion of this world. Not only have we lost our sense of Unity with the Source of our Being, but the majority has also lost its sense of Unity with its fellow beings, so that this rush towards material comfort and possessions takes into account the well-being neither of our fellow beings nor of the Earth that sustains us. The consequences of this do not rest with government alone, but with every consuming human being on this planet.

This is why, ultimately, I have put the major emphasis of this book on individual growth, as we cannot expect government to change until we change. We forget that the purpose of government is to serve its people; by our apathy and our materialism, we have allowed government to serve itself and by seeing government in terms of the illusion of our present 'economic system', we have given Money a power of its own.

I say illusion, as I have yet to be persuaded that the so-called 'science' of economics is anything but a clever jumbling of numbers to hide the fact that our present system of money and wealth exists primarily to institutionalize inequality and to maintain the status quo of those who control this wealth and thereby control the human population of this world.

From the very beginning of our evolution, the growth of our possessions and populations have been bound together with inequality, and the material gap between the rich and poor will continue to increase, as long as we live in a world which is based upon separation rather than Unity. Moreover, we shall continue to destroy our environment as long as we see the material world as the only reality and fill our lives with material goods which drain the natural resources of our planet. (I find it extremely ironic that the greatest focus of material consumption is Christmas, and if this was taken away, the whole Western economy would collapse!)

All of this, I would hope, is fairly self-evident to any concerned individual, but what does not seem to be fully understood is the extent of the illusion of what Aristotle called 'unnatural wealth' and the powers of control behind this illusion.

Unnatural wealth – the creation of money in order to create more money as opposed to being used as a medium of exchange – lies at the heart of our economic system. From the late Middle Ages when the merchant classes of Italy and Northern Europe created banks to 'raise money' for their endeavors, bank interest has become the center piece of economic control. As early as the year 1171, the City Council of Venice levied a forced loan of one per cent on the property of all their citizens, promising them interest at 5 per cent – all to finance the wars it was undertaking to expand its area of control and trade.

Since then, banks, whether private or government, have been responsible for the creation of money, but the question is: What do they create it out of? It is perfectly clear that a tiny percentage of the so-called wealth in the world consists of the coins and notes we have in our pockets. The huge majority is in the form of pieces of paper which are shifted from one bank to another, and we have no way of knowing where the money we borrow originates, or whether this indebtedness is actually created out of nothing in order to maintain the present hierarchy of power. What we do know is that the bulk of this 'money' is in the hands of the few.

For the essence of our present financial system is a sophisticated version of the system of indebtedness which we have inherited from the time when the first banks were created and power shifted into the hands of the new merchant class. In those early days, though, this power was still counterbalanced by the older, more established rulers who had used their own particular means of keeping the masses in check; when they fell during the Age of Revolutions and when the Industrial Revolution elevated materialism to a new plateau – only then did Money, and those who possessed it, assume absolute power.

We now find ourselves in a new kind of tyranny in which the average person puts in his or her 40 hour week to eke out an existence in enslavement through indebtedness to credit cards, mortgages, loans etc. This is increasingly encouraged by the banks, so that we may buy all the material things we like and continue this destructive cycle. And indebtedness does not stop there. Every country has a huge national debt, not least of all, the most prosperous of all, the United States of America. But, do we know to whom are we indebted?

What this goes to show is that the real credit of a community or a nation – in other words, the people within it and their creativity – is, in our present system, subsidiary to the artificial credit of artificial money. We are driven forward by the notion that wealth can only be created if the gross national product of a country is continuously increasing and that, without this increase, the whole fabric of our lives will collapse. We have somehow been deluded into equating the wealth of our lives with material wealth, rather than seeing in terms of the richness of human experience. We have come to accept work as a means of 'making a living' rather than as a true expression of our creativity.

If everyone continues to believe this lie, the powers of control which maintain this illusion will continue to dominate our lives. As has been the case for centuries, this hierarchy of control is the essence of separation, working on the principle of divide and rule – and its means of separation is money and the promotion of the materialist ethic which has so successfully smothered the spiritual, connective nature of our species.

Only if we see through this illusion and reclaim our power and responsibility will we be able to create change in our society. One only has to look at the collapse of the seemingly immutable Soviet system to understand that government based on separation and repressive control cannot survive for ever. When such a government falls, a comparison that always comes to my mind is the eruption of a volcano with millions of disparate energies fermenting beneath the surface, building up such pressure that an explosion is inevitable – an inevitability which is not evident from above the surface.

Although the change in the Soviet Union was effectively brought to a crisis point by only a small number of people, the desire to see the end of the old way was an energy which had built up deep within the repressed psyche of the nation as a whole. In the West, we have for so long arrogantly assumed that our 'capitalist' system is so much fairer and freer than 'communist' rule, without understanding that the duality of 'left' and 'right' is just part of the same totalitarian reality, and that we have failed to look critically within the framework of our own society. The powers which control the world of Money used the separation between the communist and capitalist worlds to focus the fear of Western man towards the 'evil enemy' in the East. Now, it is time to look within and see that our Western governments' insistence on money and increased production is an enslavement which is less obvious, but more insidious than the former totalitarian control of the Communist states.

Once again, it all comes down to individual responsibility. The Eastern European countries will be great teachers for us. What has fundamentally happened there is that responsibility has been thrust more than ever into the hands of the masses without violent revolution. In the initial stages of this major transformation, there will undoubtedly be many instances of the baser instincts of separation manifesting themselves, as different ethnic groups fight against each other. There may well even be a drift again towards totalitarian rule if the average man decides he does not wish to assume responsibility after all, but would rather have decisions made for him even if certain basic freedoms are denied. For them, it is a matter of choice; the masses are to show how they decide to use the great gift of free will.

For us in the West, we have not yet reached that stage. We allow all the fundamental political and social decisions to be made for us. We submit to the controls of the capitalist ethic, even if we feel unfulfilled by it deep down within our being. We have not yet woken up to the possibility of a new type of existence which is not bound by the treadmill of material production. We listen to our politicians campaigning, and are fed up by it all, but the masses still accept that elections are all to do with how much money we have in our pockets, rather than about the fundamental integrity of our society. As long as we really believe that this is the best kind of existence that we can hope for, then this is the best kind of existence that we will get, and, however much we grumble, this is the best kind of existence we deserve.

It is time to take a stand! It is time to acknowledge that we have spiritual, emotional, mental needs as well as material needs. It is time to accept our innate creativity and to reject the petty and intolerant view of the world which has come to govern our modern mentality. It is time to understand that the time for change has come.

There are two levels on which this change can be set in motion. The first, and ultimately most important, is on the personal level, which is why most of the second part of this book has been devoted to the ways in which we can bring Unity into our own lives. Unless we change ourselves, we cannot expect to be able to create change within others; once we do begin our own process of change, this will necessarily affect those closest to us and beyond. From this base, we will gradually find ourselves in the position where we draw towards us other people of like mind, and, as Christ said, where even two people gather together in His name, His Consciousness will expand. A few individuals become a small group, which becomes a small community, and so on. One can never underestimate the power of Love.

The second level is one of reforming government itself. Whereas the personal is the base of the pyramid, government is its apex, and, of course, the one is connected to the other. This link is particularly strong in a world of Unity, where government is not a rigid, monolithic structure out of touch with the people it governs, but a fluid basis for cooperation which works on as small a scale as possible.

Here we return to the essence of democracy: government by and for the people. This has nothing to do with the illusion of democracy which we have now in our Western world, but is based on the commitment of the people to take responsibility for the society they live in – something which can only be achieved if the responsibility for governing is devolved to smaller, individual communities.

The aim is ultimately to foster a sense of Unity which is reflected both within the macrocosm of the whole world and the microcosm of individual communities. On the broadest level, this means accepting the fact that the world of rational consciousness is a world of inequality and making this work for the good of all people by recognizing that inequality does not mean that one person is superior to or more deserving than another. We are all equal in God's eyes.

This means that the individual uses his talents as much as possible for the good of the whole while also exploring the limits of his or her own consciousness and experience. The inequality of our world can be a source of infinite delight and diversity if we appreciate our differences and do not judge what at first may seem alien to us. The resources of this world are there for us all to share, and there should never be any need for poverty or deprivation on any level.

In appreciating this diversity, we explore our own local heritage and customs, but do not fence ourselves within nationalist or tribal boundaries. There are no boundaries within a Family of Man which sees Unity in all things, and there is therefore no place for nationalism or any mentality which sets one race or country above another; nor is there any room for people or institutions who exploit other people in order to create wealth for themselves.

The greatest failing of government is to have become so all-encompassing and unwieldy that it cannot deal effectively with even the smallest problem. In its present form, it cannot change. As soon as any new idea or movement is absorbed into the monolithic structure that government has now become, it is effectively suffocated for the simple reason that it is immediately cut off from the breath of fresh air which created the initial momentum of change in the first place.

Our whole attitude towards government needs to be transformed, and, in order to do this, we must alter our whole attitude towards money and wealth. We cannot continue to despoil our planet in order to perpetuate this myth of ever increasing production. While all living men and women have a basic right to the material necessities for survival, we all

212

know deep down that our obsessive drive to increase our wealth does not fulfil our inner selves, but rather draws us away from experiencing the totality of our being and from the love and compassion we feel towards our fellow man.

It is government and the men behind it who perpetuate this illusion of endless economic growth. Economics is defined in the dictionary as 'the practical science of the production and distribution of wealth'. In reality, it is not a science at all. Not only has it been quite unable to produce a systematic consensus on how to produce wealth, but it has also hardly even addressed the question of its fair distribution. In addition, economics is built on a spurious premise: that the continuous increase of wealth is necessary for the progress of mankind.

Once we see through this illusion, the creation of a new form of government becomes a necessity. Although this is easier said than done given the reluctance of any ruling group to relinquish their power, the situation in Eastern Europe shows how even the most rigid structures of control can crumble, seemingly without warning. As I have previously stated, the pace of change on our planet at this time is a reflection of a Universal energy which is far beyond the understanding and control of our rational minds, and if enough people focus their will and actions towards creating a different environment and society based on Unity, the shadow side of separation will ultimately betray its inherent weakness, as it has no true foundation.

It is more than likely that there will have to be a major 'economic collapse' or some other crumbling of the framework of our society before the people will be galvanized into promoting this necessary change. At this time, everyone has the possibility of voting for such political parties as the Green Party whose policies recognize the fact that we are on the edge of a Crisis, yet they choose not to do so. It seems that the huge 'middle-class' has become so self-satisfied and so used to the superficiality of materialism that their fear of losing a portion of material excess through gradual social change has blinded them to the possibility of losing far more through a sudden disintegration of the material comfort and stability which they take for granted – a process which will ultimately force them to confront deeper issues within themselves.

This scenario may seem a little harsh, but it brings us back again to the fundamental question of free will and the natural balance of the Universe. If we choose to turn our backs on Unity and Love and continue to create more separation in our world to the point of going beyond that fine boundary of upsetting the balance on our planet, we must be prepared to take the consequences. Just as someone who has denied aspects of their inner lives is often faced with a serious disease in order to confront this imbalance on a deeper level, so humanity as a whole is on the verge of being confronted with greater manifestations of disharmony, if we do not choose to recreate a sense of balance and harmony ourselves.

I do not wish to sound like one of those people who gets on his soap box, declaring that the end of the world is nigh and the vengeance of an angry god is upon us. I only wish that humanity would begin to understand the basic law of balance – that every action has its consequence. With the increasing gaps in the ozone layer and virulent diseases such as AIDS which attack those very organisms within our body which are supposed to destroy viruses, the signs are there that the inner and outer layers which protect our physical being are being eroded – a process which will increase with greater intensity if humanity continues on its present path.

With this in mind, I see the major priorities of government.

First the gradual dismantling and opening up of the present banking system. As the source of power in our contemporary society is money, there can be no secrecy about it in a world of Unity, for the wealth of each nation and of the Earth as a whole can no longer be controlled by an elite class. It is now time for this wealth to be shared more equitably and to be used for the benefit of all living beings and the planet as a whole.

In a world of Unity, this does not mean wreaking vengeance on those who have exerted this control and then creating a new institution of power, as happened following the Communist Revolution in Russia. It is a matter of changing our perception towards money, and using it as a means of bridging rather than increasing the inequality in our society.

This can only be achieved if we turn away from the mentality of creating money in order to make more money, for this gives money the potential to be used as an instrument of power and control. Instead, we must abolish the whole concept of lending money for interest which has created the servitude of indebtedness in our world, and return to the original idea of money as a means of exchange, whereby it is used for the benefit of individual communities rather than immense institutions.

I am sure that successive governments, even if they wanted to do so, have not taken such radical steps because they recognized that the resulting scandals and loss in confidence would bring about an economic collapse for which they would be held responsible. This would take more selfless courage than exists within our present generation of politicians, even if they had the desire to uncover the power wielded by the great financial institutions.

Despite the reverberations of such an act, it is much more sensible to deal with the present financial system consciously and openly rather than allow it to run its course and collapse without any forewarning or preparation. If the resistance of the banking community is too great and if the will of government and the people to create such change is too weak, then we shall have no choice but to surrender our power over this situation and accept the consequences.

The power of the major banks and the great multi-national companies is built on their size and the influence they wield across the spectrum of the world. The common person knows little of the individuals who wield this power; nor do most of these individuals have much contact with or consideration for the common people. The size of these institutions conceals a separation on the most extreme level between those who wield power and their subjects.

In a society built on Unity, there cannot exist such impersonal, huge institutions, as they cannot be part of a true, participatory democracy. The essence of democracy in its purest form is that individual communities take as much responsibility for the running of their own affairs as possible, and having a large organization with headquarters far away dominating such a community is not feasible.

It is a natural part of Unity that those who put their labor into an organization should participate in its running, and organizational or industrial democracy is therefore an integral part of democracy as a whole. This takes a commitment to Unity on all sides. From the point of view of those who have controlled the organizations, this means ceding much of this control to the people employed by them. From the workers' standpoint, this means that they can no longer be apathetic and grumble about their conditions, but must actively participate in the decision making process. Both must overcome generations of conditioning and I do not underestimate the changes in mentality that they require.

Such individual participation and devolution of power is a necessary part of the true democratic process as a whole, the purpose of which is to nurture an environment based on Unity and Love.* All material considerations are a reflection of this.

This is most easily achieved within the smaller scope of individual communities so that all the material aspects of government may come under the responsibility of those whom they affect most closely. In this way, the running of banking, education, housing, health, etc. is always accountable to the community served. Every individual is encouraged to participate on some level; those who choose not to are fundamentally making the choice not to have any say in how their lives are run.

This is where the question of work comes in. In recent times, we have been so indoctrinated in this illusion of greater and greater productivity that we have come to accept that it is our duty to work forty hours a week until we retire. This in itself is an illusion.

For one thing, there is not one industrialized Western country that has full employment. For another, there will be less employment in the traditional sense when this cycle of continuously producing more and more unnecessary goods comes to an end.

Traditional economists would shudder in horror at the idea of purposely reducing consumption, but, in reality, this can only improve the quality of life — not only in terms of the pollution we spew out into our atmosphere, but also with regard to the way we view Work.

The current direction of education, which is to aim the student towards a particular job or profession, is bound

---

*In a world of Unity, politicians assume responsibility because of their desire to serve rather than for their own power or material wealth, and therefore, as Plato intimated, do not need any special material reward.

within the narrow confines of a purely materialistic world view, dependent on increased productivity. Within a world of Unity, however, work is quite simply the expression of an individual's creativity. This may certainly include the ability to participate in creating material objects, but it may just as well pertain to a particular talent which will benefit the community in a non-material way.

If there is less production in this world, then people will be able to spend more time and energy on projects which have more to do with human values and the necessities of life, such as caring for the elderly and disadvantaged, keeping the physical infrastructures of communities in shape, looking after the land. Women will be able to be more flexible and spend time with their children; there will be more time and space for community based projects which will not be intent on making a profit, but will serve the needs of the people living in the community.

Every person has the right to work for as long as he or she is able to without being enslaved to a job. In the world of diversity and inequality that exists today, there will always be people who are better equipped to do certain types of work than others, but, in a world of Unity, people do not use their intellect and rational powers to raise themselves up above other people, but recognize the necessity of serving the greater purpose of the Whole.

The great technology we have in our hands can be used to eliminate as many dirty and boring jobs as possible, while also being harnessed to explore alternative means of producing energy which do not disrupt the natural balance of our planet. It goes without saying that the emphasis of any form of government is to re-establish this balance and focus on all sustainable ways of life, ranging from education about population control and agricultural methods to the husbanding of our natural resources and the reduction of pollution.

The natural inequality I have just mentioned also necessitates the concept of a Global Community. Unity and cooperation are of no use if just confined to certain parts of the world, and it is our global responsibility to see that sharing exists on every level. Global Community is the antithesis of the present division between the rich nations and the Third World; it is the rich sharing with rather than exploiting the poor; it is the understanding that nobody needs to go hungry or be forced into a modern industrial life if they wish to keep to their old traditions; but, equally, it is up to each community, rich or poor, to create its own sense of Unity, rather than focusing on the divisions of the past.

It means also accepting, as native people still do throughout the world, that no individual or group can own land. The Earth is the common heritage of all living people and is there for all to share. This does not give any person the right to invade another person's home, for humanity is, after all, a predominantly settled race, but this equally does not give any person the right to control tracts of land for the sole purpose of making money out of them.

Finally, the essential point of any democracy is to protect the rights and freedom of the individual. Democracy, in its present form of the majority winning outright, takes minimal account of minorities. Our modern democratic society still emphasizes the need to conform, rather than encouraging free individual expression and exploration. It pays lip service to minorities, but whether they are racial, religious or sexual, society still exhibits prejudice towards them both in day to day life or backed by the weight of law. If we cannot overcome prejudice towards our neighbor, how can we begin to create a world of Unity on a larger scale?

From a politician's point of view, I have no doubt that this vision of a true democracy would seem vague and impractical, but, in any climate of profound change, the essence of any transformation is not the mechanics of it but the will and the mentality behind it.

Nobody knows the exact pace or nature of the changes that are ahead of us. I believe that they are going to be so immense that we will no longer be able to be bound by the way the past few generations have perceived the world. If I wrote more specifically on such material considerations as taxation which seem to obsess Western man, I would not only be exceeding the limits of this book and of my own knowledge, but I would also be projecting an image of what the nature of our society will be at the millennium.

The whole point of any period of major transformation is that it is a waste of time trying to look into the future, in particular from a perspective which is conditioned by the past. The future will unfurl from the actions of the present, and all we can do is to project into our own present thoughts and actions what we perceive as being the Truth. If enough people act according to the principles of Unity, then, at some point, this Unity will spread throughout our world, even into the darkest recesses of government.

Chapter 8

Reconciliation and Transformation

I have no doubt that many would see this vision of government and democracy as unrealistic and idealistic, but they do not take into account the power of the changes which are beginning to reshape our world.

The era when continuous economic growth was taken for granted is now in the past. There will be some who assert that the current recession is a mild hiccup, but the closer they are to the center of government, the more they know that they are deluding themselves and the people they govern. The current system is so rotten on the inside, so eaten away by greed and lack of concern for the Whole, that its very fabric is close to collapse. The longer the economic slowdown lasts, the barer the threads that bind the system together will become, until the illusion of the premise upon which it is built will be there for all to see.

It is of course possible, even probable, that people will remain blind because they do not wish to see what is going on, in which case a major internal collapse or some external force will be required to stimulate the change which is inevitable — at which point, the masses of the Western world are going to be faced with the fundamental choice which is now facing Eastern Europe: whether to draw together in this crisis or whether to lash out in fear at one's neighbor or at those we see as being responsible for it.

The people of Eastern Europe have been liberated from an oppression in which they had few material comforts, so the appreciation of this liberation preceded the clamor for greater material benefits. In the West, the majority have lived in comfort for years and those who did not experience the World Wars have known nothing else. Therefore, when the crisis comes into our homes, it will not be perceived as the gaining of freedom, but the loss of material security. The fear and disruption which this will engender will create a much greater potential conflict than in the East. Eastern Europeans have at least been bound together by what they perceive as material lack; Western culture, on the other hand, has encouraged the ethos of competition and personal ambition, so we would not be so conditioned to draw together in such a crisis. (In the World Wars, however, we did just that, because we were facing a common enemy. Yet, in this crisis, there will be no discernible enemy, and we shall therefore be confronted by nothing but ourselves, our own nature.)

Any fundamental collapse of the old is a wonderful opportunity to herald in a new era of greater enlightenment, but history has shown again and again how the traumatic shock of such sudden change creates an energy of fear and panic which sweeps away the strength and vision to build a new, higher consciousness.

I believe that, this time around, it can be different, as long as we prepare ourselves for the change to come rather than deny that it can ever happen to us; at the very core of this shift in mentality is that we come to an understanding that we as a species can survive on this planet only if we integrate Unity and Love into every fabric of our being.

The reason I am so optimistic is that, in the midst of the greed and apathy which exists in our modern world, I have over the past few years seen more and more people going through intense crises in their own lives which have forced them to go deep within themselves and gradually create a raising of their consciousness. For nearly all of us (for I include myself in this), it has been an arduous and often painful struggle; yet out of this has come a greater sense of our own identity and a deeper compassion for others who are going through their own painful changes.

This does not mean that those who have created change in their lives and found their own God Within are in any way superior to those who have chosen to continue conforming to the precepts of society. It simply means that they have discovered their inner strength to guide others along their path of discovery. There is no right or wrong way of following this path.

We are about to enter a period of reconciliation on every level of our existence, and, just as in the opposition between Horus and Set, conflict and strife will exist before this reconciliation can take place. The whole point of the crisis which is going to overtake our lives is that the unnatural constraints which we have borne for so long are going to be swept away, and each and every one of us is going to face the test of how we assume the responsibility of using our own free will in this new world without anyone being able to make the decisions for us.

I cannot say how long this process will take, as I do not know the true power of our dark side which has been divorced for so long from the Unity of our Being. We all cannot fail to notice that there is much unresolved hatred, anger, fear and guilt in this world, and this energy will not just disappear when the old system crumbles. Indeed, with the old constraints removed, there may well be a period when these suppressed emotions will explode in all their ferocity, and I would be deceitful if I were to deny that the result of this could well be the violent expression of the basest human instincts in many segments of our society. But, the dark side of separation can play itself out only if the deep, pent up feelings caused by it can find a natural release – and, unless we are able to find ways in which to let the air out slowly, the pressure will build up until the balloon bursts with one cathartic bang.

It is for this reason that I believe it is time to begin to relearn the importance of ritual – not in the pompous form of modern religious ceremony, but as a primal experience where the elemental energies of man and woman are able to be released within the safety of a harmonious group.

In is excellent book, *The Magic Of Ritual*, Tom Driver points out the three purposes of ritual: creating and preserving order; fostering community; effecting transformation. We have of course seen how the first of these has held sway for centuries in the Judaic, Islamic and Christian religions to the virtual exclusion of the last, and, in doing so, these hypocrites have betrayed the true spiritual nature of man and women in order to preserve their own temporal power.

I have had some harsh words to say about those who govern us, but, for me, the greatest sadness is the way that these religions have abused their power to deny the masses their spiritual heritage. Of course, there are many wonderful people today working within the framework of these religions who are trying to return to the simple message of Love; Tom Driver himself devotes his final chapter to restoring the true power of ritual to the Christian sacraments. Yet, such men and women are a small minority within the rigid hierarchies of these religions, and I believe that the power of spirit and of ritual must primarily be recreated outside of these structures in order to meet the needs of the people and to create transformation on the large scale which will be required in the coming years.

If combined with fostering community and effecting transformation, the making and preservation of order through ritual can be a powerful, creative force in that the violence which has become so endemic in our society can be transmuted into an energy of positive change.

I have always found absurd the fashionable theories of modern anthropologists that man is a naturally violent and aggressive creature, for they do not begin to address the fact that this aggression is quite simply a result of our elemental energies being cut off from the 'natural' Unity between all living beings and with the Whole of which the Earth is a microcosm. Their materially bound speculation is so typical of all kinds of philosophical inquiry of our modern age, in that it denies the essential good of all living things and tries to rationalize the aspects of our behavior which we judge as being 'bad'.

Ritual is the age-old method of channeling the elemental energies of mankind. The frenzy of ritual, as practiced in so-called 'less civilized' religions, may appear to our 'refined senses' to be the very antithesis of order in that there appears to be no outside means of control, but, in reality, its elemental power creates a naturally binding order which is intrinsically more stable than the artificial, intellectually based ceremonies of modern, Western religion.

The essence of ritual, through the transformative power of sound and movement, is to take groups of men and women to a realm beyond our physical, day-to-day reality, where all the divisions of the rational mind disappear and all the elements of strife merge into a well of Unity. Within this Unity, the individual and the group are one and yet retain their own identity, for the power of ritual is that it emotionally binds the group together and at the same time permits each individual to experience his or her personal connection to the Whole within the safety of the group setting. The creation and preservation of order is actually no more than a natural result of this process, rather than an end in itself. By failing to understand this and placing its primary emphasis on order, orthodox religions have managed to create boring rituals devoid of any elemental power.

I have only experienced a powerful ceremonial ritual once in Egypt, yet I have experienced the same energy many times in one of the few settings where such elemental, ritual power is released in our contemporary Western society: the disco, the writhing, charged atmosphere of which differs from ancient ritual only in that the majority of its participants are letting off steam rather than consciously harnessing its energy as a means of inner transformation.

I believe that the emergence of disco with its elemental beat is responding to the need of young people living in a dense, material world to connect with something deep and unifying within themselves in an anarchic environment where there is no external authority in sight. The fact that recreational drugs are used in these spaces is no coincidence too, for natural, hallucinogenic plants are often used to create the impetus for transformation in many ancient rituals – the major difference being that Westerners are not initiated to understand the immense power, both creative and destructive, which these substances have.

Now, I am not suggesting that we all go to the disco and take drugs! What I am proposing is that, whatever kind of community we live in, we find a way of recreating ritual within this community. It may be in the form of a revitalized Christian ceremony, or we may wish to study Native American or other ancient rituals which re-establish our connection to the Earth and its cycles, or it may be something which arises spontaneously from the exploration of sound, music, movement and dance through the mediation of a modern day shaman – male or female. The knowledge of ritual is deeply implanted within every living being, and more and more people are beginning to tap into this ancient well of knowledge. It is now time to unleash this force in order to create an environment for the spiritual liberation of the masses, as opposed to the elitist approach which exists today even in some of the more enlightened spiritual organizations.

Even if this is begun in the smallest groups, the nucleus for change can gradually be expanded. As individuals discover the shaman within themselves, they can begin to invoke the powers which lie behind what we perceive as the physical, the only real world. Some will find that the liberation and transformation they undergo through this deeper connection to the essence of their being will bring out their leadership – not a leadership of privileged authority, but, like the Druids of old, a leadership which integrates the temporal, material world with the eternal world of Spirit in which we all live together in harmony and balance with each other and the world around us.

Leadership is needed as humanity goes through a major shift in consciousness, but there is no space for elitism in this new world of Unity. No true leader needs to have material privileges, as the sense of feeling connected to the Whole and of being of service to others is a gift in and of itself – and in the end, the leader's job is only complete when every living man and woman is ready to assume their own responsibility for themselves and their community, so that leadership is required no more.

So, finally, we come back again to what I mentioned in the Introduction: this book is all about responsibility. If we wish to see change take place in this world of ours, it is no good sitting back and waiting for others to set the ball rolling. The impetus must come from every part of the world and from every segment of society – an impetus which needs to start from within, with reconciliation and transformation on every level of our own individual being, so that this may ultimately expand to be reflected in the world at large.

I do not say that following such a path will be easy, as there will undoubtedly be much resistance as people cling on to the old ways of power and control, mainly through fear. But that is part of the challenge. If you look deep within yourself, do you really want to continue living a life in which you are barely touching your innate creativity and strength, or do you wish to explore beyond the limits of the dictates of a fearful society and contribute to the creation of an environment where people can freely express their own true nature? The choice is yours.

Along this expansive path, faith and patience will be your greatest allies: faith in your own divine nature which allows you to surrender to your own inner guidance, and patience in the knowledge that all will resolve itself in its own time if you follow this guidance of your heart.

And, ultimately, this will lead to a Unity within your own being. The strife and challenges of duality, which at times may seem to have been the only kind of environment which you have experienced, will have fulfilled their purpose: to expand your consciousness to new dimensions, so that the Unity to which you return is greater and deeper than the Unity from which you emerged those millennia ago.

Duality is the action of becoming.

Unity is the peace of being.

Bibliography

ARISTOTLE. *Complete Works*.

BAMFORTH, NICK. *AIDS and The Healer Within*, Amethyst Books, London/New York, 1987.
Trusting The Healer Within, Amethyst, 1989.
What on Earth is Happening? with Denise Cooney and Eric Morse, Amethyst, 1991.

CAMPBELL, JOSEPH. *The Masks of God*, Viking Penguin New York/London
1. *Primitive Mythology*, 1959.
2. *Oriental Mythology*, 1962.
3. *Occidental Mythology*, 1964.

CAPRA, FRITJOF. *The Tao of Physics*, Shambala, Boston.

DRIVER, TOM F. *The Magic of Ritual*, Harper Collins, San Francisco, 1991.

FINLEY, M.I. (ed.)., *The Legacy of Greece*, Oxford University Press, 1981.

The Green Party Manifesto. London.

JAYNES, JULIAN. *The Origin of Consciousness in the Break-down of the Bicameral Mind*, Houghton Mifflin, Boston, 1982.

KEE, ALISTAIR. *Constantine versus Christ*, SCMP, London.

LAROUSSE. *World Mythology*, Hamlyn, London/New York, 1965.

MORSE, ERIC. *The Living Stars*, Amethyst, London/New York, 1988.

PERRY, JULIAN (ed.). *Mindweld: A Cosmic Embrace*, Amethyst, 1991.

PLATO. *Complete Works*.

RAIGUEL, JILL. *The Next Step: A Life Skills Workbook for Adult Survivors of Emotional Abuse*, Amethyst, 1991.

RUSSELL, BERTRAND. *Wisdom of the West*, Rathbone, London, 1959.

SCHWALLER DE LUBICZ, R.A. *The Temple of Man*, tr. R. & D. Lawtor, Inner Traditions, New York, 1977.

STEWART, R.J. *The Mystic Life of Merlin*, Routledge & Kegan Paul, London/New York, 1986.

WEST, JOHN ANTHONY. *The Traveler's Key to Ancient Egypt*, Alfred A. Knopf, New York, 1985.

WILLIAMS, WALTER L. *The Spirit and The Flesh: Sexual Diversity in American Indian Culture*, Beacon Press, Boston, 1986.

ZUKAV, GARY. *The Dancing Wu Li Masters*, William Morrow, New York, 1979.

Index

Abel, 161
Aborigines, 44, 199
abortion, 188
Abraham, 99
Achilles, 71
Adam & Eve, 17, 19, 161
Aeolians, 72
Africa, 23
Ahura Mazda, 74
AIDS, 27, 159-160, 176-8, 214
alchemy, 117
Alexander the Great, 67, 69, 93, 95
Alexandria, 101
America, 53, 110, 128, 130, 209
American, native, 58, 177, 199, 225
Amon, 65
anarchy, 205
Anatolia, 72
Anaxagoras, 78, 80, 102
Anaximander, 76
Anaximanes, 75
Angra Mainyu, 74
Aphrodite, 81
Apollo, 70, 77
Arabia, 99, 115

arete, 71, 168
aries, age of, 65
Aristotle, 82, 85, 86, 90-4, 96, 109, 119-120, 121, 180
Arthurian legends, 114, 116
Aryans, 70, 99, 130
Ashoka, 98
ataraxia, 95
Athena, 70
Athens, 73, 78-95
Atlantis, 16, 23, 111, 161-2
atomists, 78, 95, 124, 149
Aztecs, 51, 110

'ba', 58, 60
Babylon, 99
banking system, 119-120, 208, 214-5
Berkeley, 126
Bismarck, 129, 130
Black Death, 119
Book of the Dead, 58
Bosch, 122
Britain, 25, 110-14, 116, 125-7, 199
Buddha, 19, 74, 79, 97-8, 100
Byzantium, 109, 115

Cain, 161
Calvin, 123
Calypso, 72
Cambyses, 66
Campbell, Joseph, 17, 19, 32, 39, 48
Candide, 127
capitalism, 129-130, 210
Cartesian philosophy, 124, 125
catastrophe theory, 23, 29
Catholocism, 122-3
Celts, 111, 112
chance, 149-150, 189
Charlemagne, 108, 128
Chaucer, 115
childhood, 161, 165, 188-204
China, 79, 110
Chrétien de Troyes, 116
Christ, the man, 74, 97-105, 116-17, 157, 167, 169, 211
Christ Consciousness, 98, 101-5, 111, 112, 156-7, 211
Christian Church, 19, 61, 87, 103-111, 112, 114-16, 122-6, 167, 175, 177
Christianity, 59, 61-2, 67, 69, 83, 90, 97-111, 112, 114-17, 177, 185, 224, 225
Christmas, 208
Circe, 72
city-states, 42-3, 47ff, 69, 73, 80, 99
Cleopatra, 67
Clovis, 108
Columbus, 120
communism, 210, 214
Confucius, 79
Constantine, 67, 98, 103
Copernicus, 122
Council of Nicaea, 67, 103, 115
courtly love, 114-15

creation myths, 15ff, 100, 161
Crete, 47, 53, 55, 69-70

Damascus, 101
Darius, 1 66, 74
Darwin, 129
Delphi, 70
democracy, 80, 82, 88, 93, 131, 206, 211-12, 215-18, 221
Descartes, 123, 125, 126, 127, 149
dharma, 17, 57
dialectics, 83, 89, 95, 200-1
Diocletian, 103
DNA, 149
Dominicans, 110
Dorians, 71-2
Druids, 112, 226
dualism,
  dark/light, 32, 61-2, 74, 91, 130, 157-170, 174-5
  East/West, 17-20, 34, 48, 67, 70, 73-4, 76, 79, 86, 98, 107, 109, 116
  God/man, 16-20, 47-54, 98, 105, 122-4, 150-1, 153, 199
  good/evil, 61-2, 74, 91-2, 100, 104, 131, 148, 155-170
  health/disease, 76, 91, 151, 159-160, 176-7
  immutable/fluid, 78, 84, 86, 120, 122, 124, 139-141, 145-150, 206-7, 209-211
  individual/group, 31, 34-6, 51-4, 66, 75, 80-1, 93, 110, 127, 195-7, 215-18, 223-5
  life/death, 31-2, 37-40, 48, 51-2, 58-60, 62, 95, 114, 116, 137-144, 181
  macrocosm/microcosm, 35, 48, 145-154, 202

male/female, 17, 36-40, 48-51,
63-4, 70-1, 80-1, 91, 113-16,
168, 174, 179-182
mind/body/(spirit), 73, 77, 81,
86-7, 91, 102, 123-4, 172-5
North/South, 70, 107-8, 111-12,
114, 122-3, 125
objective/subjective, 87, 148
order/chaos, 43, 53, 57, 64-5,
93, 107, 148-150, 205-7, 224-
5
rational/intuitive, 25ff, 47-50,
57-8, 62-4, 83, 89, 94, 102,
121, 142, 148-9, 152, 167-8,
196-204
reason/revelation, 16, 109, 120
rich/poor, 45, 74, 104, 110,
208, 217-18
spiritual/material, 28, 34, 44,
51-2, 58, 65-6, 75, 77-8, 91,
94-5, 102-5, 110, 116-17, 141,
143, 172-5, 181-2, 191, 209,
226
duality and fear, 17-20, 31-2, 34,
39, 50, 54, 101, 130-3, 142-3,
149, 161, 168, 176, 222-3, 226
duality and guilt, 17-20, 25, 39,
50, 131, 143, 158, 161, 163-6,
171, 175-8, 223
duality as a creative force, 19,
50, 60-3, 76, 86, 98, 158-160,
201, 227
Dürer, 122

earth energies, 31, 33, 35, 37-40,
43-4, 48-9, 51, 70, 111-13, 153-4,
156, 168, 172, 180-1, 225
economics, 119, 207, 219, 221
education, 83, 88-9, 95-6, 195-
204, 216-17
ego, 18, 45, 128, 158-160, 163

Egypt, 43, 47, 53, 55-68, 69, 71,
73-4, 76-7, 81, 86, 93, 101, 102,
122, 128, 158, 162, 180, 225
Eleanor of Aquitaine, 115
Eleatic philosophers, 78-9
elements, 76, 113
Empedocles, 76, 201
empiricists, 125-7
England, 126, 128, 129
Epicureanism, 95
Erasmus, 122
Eros, 81
'eudaimonia', 92
Euphrates river, 47

'fall' of man, 16ff, 74, 161
female power, 17, 20, 28, 36-40,
48-51, 57, 60, 63, 70-1, 99, 113-
15, 168, 174, 180-2
feudalism, 64, 107-9, 114, 119,
130
First World War, 130
Fisher King, 117
France, 115, 128
Franciscans, 110
Franks, 108
French Revolution, 128

gaia principle, 145
Galahad, 116
Galileo, 110, 122, 147
Ganieda, 113, 114, 181
Garden of Eden, 16ff, 38, 161
Geb, 59
Genesis, 15ff
Geoffrey of Monmouth, 112
Germany, 108, 116, 119, 123, 130,
168
gnostics, 61-2, 101, 103
Goddess, 20, 36-40, 48-51, 57,
60, 70-2, 91, 99, 111, 113, 115,

174
government, 11, 43, 52, 80-1, 87-8, 93, 157, 168-9, 205-219, 221
Grail, 44, 114, 116-17, 120
Greece, 23, 67, 69-96, 97, 99, 101-4, 109, 116-17, 122, 124, 143, 149, 162, 168, 180, 196, 200, 205
Greek gods, 19, 58, 70-1, 78, 99
greenhouse effect, 154
Green Party, 200, 213
Grunewald, 122
Guendolena, 113, 114, 181
Guenevere, 114
Guillaume IX, 115

Harappa, 43, 47, 53, 55, 70
Hathor, 57
Hegel, 129
Heliopolitan Ennead, 59, 60, 63
Hellenism, 94-6, 101-2
Heraclitus, 75-6, 86, 201
heresy, 61-2, 103, 109, 116
Hermes, 19
hieroglyphs, 56-8
Hinduism, 23, 97
Hippocrates, 76
Hitler, 130
holocaust, 130, 168
Holy Ghost, 102, 104
Holy Grail, see Grail
Homer, 71-2, 73, 89
homosexuality, 177-9
Horus, 59-61, 63, 66, 143, 158, 223
humanism, 83, 120, 126
Hume, 124, 126-7
Hyksos, 65

Irnhotep, 62
Incas, 51, 110

India, 17, 79, 110
Indus river, 47
Industrial revolution, 129-130, 209
Ionia, 72-5, 77, 79, 96
Ireland, 25, 110, 199
iron age, 53, 66
Isis, 59-60, 158
Islam, 109, 110, 115, 175, 177, 224
Italy, 78, 119-122, 208

Judaism, 97, 99-101, 104, 115, 168, 175, 177, 224
Judeo-Christian mentality, 15-16, 39, 91, 160
Julius Caesar, 112
Jung, 16, 40, 110, 117, 161, 180

'ka', 58, 60
Kabbalah, 76, 115
Karnak, 65
Kepler, 122
Khepri, 58
Khonsu, 65
King Rhydderich, 113
kings, as God, 62, 87-8, 128; sacrifice of, 51-2
Knossos, 71
'kundalini', 19, 172

Lancelot, 114
language, 29-31, 35, 41
'langue d'oc', 115
Lascaux cave paintings, 33
Lemuria, 161-2
Leonardo da Vinci, 121, 198
Leucippus, 78
Levant, 19, 48, 70
ley lines, 111
liberalism, 125, 128-130
Locke, 126, 128

'logos', 102
Louis XIV, 128
Louis XVI, 128
Louis Napoléon, 129
love as unifying force, 20, 76, 98, 101, 115, 156-171, 181, 184, 192-3, 197, 201, 211, 216, 222
Lug, 113, 117
Luther, 123
Luxor, 65

Maat, 57, 58, 60, 180
male domination, 20, 36-8, 49-51, 58-9, 63-4, 70-1, 80-1, 91, 94, 99, 114, 117, 168, 174, 181, 192
Mallory, 116
Manilus, 23
Marathon, 79
Marduk, 99
marriage, 81, 114, 174, 185-8
materialist philosophy, 78-83, 91-6, 126-8
mathematics, 47, 56, 62-3, 76-7, 89, 122, 198
'maya', 86, 98, 140
Mediterranean, 71, 73, 99
Medusa, 70
Memphis, 63
Menes, 56
Merlin, 112-14, 116, 181
Mesopotamia, 55, 66, 69, 72, 74, 99
Michelangelo, 121, 198
Middle Ages, 37, 48, 90, 107-117, 119, 120, 121, 199, 208
middle-platonists, 102
Miletus, 73-4, 78, 126
Min-Amon, 65
Minoan civilization, 69-72
Mongols, 110

monotheism, 20, 74, 91
moon, 20, 29, 59, 112, 168, 180
Moslem, see Islam
Mount Olympus, 78
Mount Sinai, 25
music, 77, 89, 112-13, 115, 130, 198, 225
Mut, 65
Mycaenae, 71-2
myth 15ff; see also Greek gods, Osiris, Middle Ages etc
myth and education, 89, 198-9, 202

Napoléon, 128-9
Narmer Palette, 57
nationalism, 129-130, 212
Neanderthal man, 32
Nefertum, 63
Nehemiah, 100
neolithic culture, 39, 48, 55
neo-platonists, 102
Newton, 110, 122, 147, 151
Noah, 23, 162
nomadic tribes, 31-6, 43-4, 70-1, 99, 156
Nonnos, 23
'nous', 78, 102
numerology, 60
Nun, 59

Odin, 113, 117
Odyssey, 71-2
Old Testament, 15ff, 66, 99, 156
Omphalos, 70
Orpheus, 77
Orphic religion, 73, 77, 89
Osiris, 59-61, 158
Ovid, 23
ozone layer, 154, 214

π & ø, 62, 65
Pakistan, 47
Paleolithic tombs, 38
Pan, 113
parenthood, 165, 186-193
Parmenides, 78, 86, 124
Paul of Tarsus, 101
Peloponnesian War, 79
Perceval, 116-17
Pericles, 80, 85, 207
Perseus, 70
Persia, 66-7, 74, 79, 100, 101
Phaeton, 23-5
Pharaoh, 56ff, 87-8
Philae, 67
Philo, 102
Piscean age, 110, 117, 169
Plato, 23, 82, 85-96, 102, 109, 120, 122, 201, 216
platonists, 102
Plotinus, 102
'polis', 80-1, 85, 92-4
Polynesia, 23
popes, 108, 110
pre-Socratiac philosophers, 73-9, 82, 86, 91, 94, 96, 122, 126
protestant church, 123
Prussia, 130
'psychic birth', 16, 40, 161
Ptah, 63
Ptolomies, 67
puberty rites, 34, 172, 197
pyramids, 62-5, 111
Pythagoras, 76-8, 83, 86, 89, 122, 198

quantum mechanics, 78, 145-7, 149

rational mind, birth of, 23ff

Re, 58, 63
reality, nature of, 145-9
Reformation, 120, 122-3
reincarnation/rebirth, 20, 32, 39-40, 48, 60, 77, 101, 103, 163
religious orthodoxy, 16, 20, 100-1, 107, 111, 120, 131, 141, 147, 153, 168, 174-5, 199, 224
Renaissance, 90, 120-2, 126, 198
resurrection, 101, 109
rhetoric, 82, 89, 95, 201
ritual, 32-5, 39-40, 44, 51-2, 103, 112, 116, 123, 188, 223-6
romanticism, 127, 130
Rome, 23, 55, 67, 69, 95, 96, 97, 103-4, 107-8, 109, 111, 112, 114, 123, 128, 162
Rousseau, 127
Russia, 70, 110, 214

sacrifice, 32, 34, 39-40, 44, 51-2, 62, 81, 113
Saqqara, 62
Satan, 19, 61, 160, 161
sceptics, 94, 124, 126-7
scholasticism, 107, 109, 115, 120
Schopenhauer, 125
Schwaller de Lubicz, 63, 65
Scotland, 111
Sekhmet, 63
self, awareness of, 17-18, 30, 38, 41, 45, 52-4, 63, 102, 160, 195-6
Semites, 99
serpent, 19-20, 24, 39, 70, 161
Set, 59-61, 143, 158-9, 160, 223
sexuality, 19, 34, 39, 63, 65, 114, 116, 139, 161, 166, 168, 171-182, 187
shaman, 32-4, 38-9, 51, 72, 113, 127, 177, 226
sin, 17, 25-7, 83, 104, 157, 165,

167, 175
Sinn Fein, 25
Socrates, 82-5, 87, 89, 92, 93, 95, 96
sophists, 82, 89, 95, 201
Soviet Union, 24, 206, 209-210
Spain, 51, 111
Spinoza, 125
stoicism, 95
Stonehenge, 111-12
sufism, 115
Sumeria, 43, 47, 48, 53, 55, 56, 99, 112, 128, 162
Synod of Whitby, 111, 112

temple, 48, 63, 65, 67, 81, 93, 98, 112, 182
Ten Commandments, 156
Thales, 74-6, 80, 126
Thatcher, 181
Thebes, 65
Theodosius, 104
Third World, 186, 217
Thomas Aquinas, 109-110, 120
Tiamat, 99
Tigris river, 47

trinity, 37-8, 59, 77, 102-4, 109, 113-14, 181-2
troubadours, 115
Troy, 71, 99
Turkey, 72

Universal Authority of the Group, 31, 34-44, 52-4, 66, 103, 107, 129, 131-2, 156, 161, 195-6, 206
Ur, 99

Venice, 208
Virgin Mary, 115
Vita Merlini, 112-14
Voltaire, 127

Wales, 111

Yahweh, 20, 99

Zeno, 78
Zeus, 70
Zoroaster, 74
Zoser, 62